Planning your Wedding

Practical books that inspire

Making a Wedding Speech
*How to face the big occasion with confidence
and carry it off with style*

Making the Father of the Bride's Speech
Etiquette – Jokes – Sample speeches – One-liners

Be the Best, Best Man & Make a Stunning Speech

Save £'000s Buying Your Home
*A step-by-step guide to reducing the price of a house
and the cost of your mortgage*

howtobooks

Please send for a free copy of the latest catalogue:

How To Books
3 Newtec Place, Magdalen Road
Oxford OX4 1RE, United Kingdom
email: info@howtobooks.co.uk
http://www.howtobooks.co.uk

Planning your Wedding

*A step-by-step guide that will take
you right through to the big day*

JUDITH VERITY

howtobooks

How To Books would like to thank Beverley and David Foster for
the wedding photography used for the cover and text.
David Foster, Tel: 01538 386403, www.weddingphotovideo.com
Beverley Foster, Tel: 01538 382933, www.weddingstorybook.co.uk

First published in 2003 by
How To Books Ltd, 3 Newtec Place,
Magdalen Road, Oxford OX4 1RE. United Kingdom.
Tel: (01865) 793806. Fax: (01865) 248780.
email: info@howtobooks.co.uk
http://www.howtobooks.co.uk

First edition 2003
Reprinted 2003

British Library Cataloguing in Publication Data
A catalogue record for this book is available from the British
Library

Cover design by Baseline Arts Ltd, Oxford
Produced for How To Books by Deer Park Productions
Typeset by PDQ Typesetting, Newcastle-under-Lyme, Staffs.
Printed and bound by Cromwell Press, Trowbridge, Wiltshire.

NOTE: The material contained in this book is set out in good faith
for general guidance and no liability can be accepted
for loss or expense incurred as a result of relying in particular
circumstances on statements made in the book. The laws and
regulations are complex and liable to change, and readers should
check the current position with the relevant authorities before
making personal arrangements.

Contents

Preface

You're probably reading this book because you're about to get married. Congratulations! If you don't read any further than this page, here's my best piece of advice up front: approach your wedding day in the spirit of fun and celebration. Most people get married nowadays because they want to. They fall in love, or maybe they decide that they are such good friends they want to grow old together. It's a free choice, nothing to do with money or family pressure or social status, so you also have a free choice about whether to have a simple civil ceremony, or a full church wedding and the party of a lifetime.

Whilst researching this book I discovered that pre-wedding couples tend to fall into two distinct categories. First there were the ones who planned the whole event like a military campaign and then didn't enjoy the day so much because their perfect plan ended up not being perfect. Second, there were the ones who told me they had just as much fun in the six months of preparation as they did on the day itself. Which category do you want to be in? It's up to you!

If you decide that finding the person you want to love for a lifetime is a good reason for the party of a lifetime, all the information you could ever need is right here.

The biggest problem with planning a wedding is the excessive amount of advice you'll find coming at you from all directions. No wonder so many couples are giving up on the whole thing and sneaking off to a tropical hideaway where they can tie the knot in peace. But if you want to share this wonderful decision you've made with your friends and family, this book is designed to give you all the information you need. And if you want more nitty gritty detail, Chapter Twelve has a comprehensive list of resources and contacts.

For some couples, planning their wedding is a very useful exercise in shared budgeting and getting to know more about each other's priorities. So good luck, have lots of fun and be sure to listen to what your partner really wants apart from you, of course.

Judith Verity

$$\left(1\right)$$

Getting Engaged

Getting engaged to your partner is perhaps the most positive commitment either of you will ever make, and the engagement period is a time when you should have fun and be sociable with both sets of friends and family. If you approach your engagement this way, planning your wedding will become a pleasure, not a chore.

When marriages often used to be arranged – or at least needed the approval of the parents of the bride and groom, engagements were an essential and very formal part of the process. This was a time for the couple to get to know each other while their parents thrashed out the financial settlements and planned a wedding that would fit their social status. An engagement was also a binding legal contract and an 'abandoned' fiancée or fiancé could sue for breach of promise.

Nowadays, when people make the decision to get married of their own accord – often after years of living together and even after having children – an engagement can seem like a pointless formality. But if you do decide to get engaged, rather than heading straight for the church or register office, an engagement can be a breathing space. It gives you time to plan and save for the wedding and time to think about how you are going to make your marriage work.

And, if you decide you want to do some of the traditional things – going down on your knees to propose, for example, or having an engagement party – it could also be a lot of fun.

TRADITIONAL ENGAGEMENTS
The following is the traditional route to becoming engaged. The points are numbered because the order is very important.

1. The groom would buy the ring *before* he proposed, or persuade his mother to give him the family engagement ring to present to the bride.

2. The groom then proposed to the bride, on bended knee of course in a suitably romantic setting and, if accepted, moved on to step 3. The bride didn't wear the ring in public until the engagement was formally announced.

3. The groom asked the bride's father for permission to marry his daughter and, if permission was given, the couple then proceeded with step 4.

4. Together, they announced their engagement to the groom's parents.

5. They arranged for the two sets of parents to meet, even if they already knew each other. It was traditional for the bridegroom's parents to invite the bride's parents to lunch or dinner to talk about the wedding.

6. The bride could at this stage give the groom a present – cufflinks were the usual option.

7. The announcement was made to relatives.

8. The announcement was made to close friends.

9. The bride's parents sent a notice to the newspapers.

10. The families organised an engagement party for the couple and their friends and relatives.

11. The bride starting wearing the ring in public.

ENGAGEMENTS TODAY

Most people don't go through quite such a formal procedure now, even if they do decide to get engaged, and you won't be frowned upon if you wear the ring in public before the notice goes into the *Times*. Engagement is a very personal decision made by just two people –

although, in fact, an engagement ring is a bigger symbol of commitment than a shared bathroom. And, of course, there's more to it than just an excuse for a diamond or two, but the diamonds do matter.

CHOOSING A RING

Only brave bridegrooms will choose a ring without any input from their fiancé-to-be. An engagement ring is supposed to be worth at least a month of the groom's salary but, if you find yourself thinking along these lines, you might want to ask yourself what the relationship is really about.

If you're the bride and you've been given a family ring, you have to accept that, as soon as your eldest son decides to get engaged, you'll have to hand it over.

ASKING EACH OTHER SOME TOUGH QUESTIONS

This is a good time for you and your partner to talk through what this engagement really means to you:

◆ Are you going to start a family and, if so, who will be the primary carer? Lots of very modern couples shy away from talking about this, although it used to be the main reason for getting married and it's still one of the major reasons for breaking up when couples can't agree about it.

◆ Whose career takes precedence in times of crisis?

◆ Do either of you want to move house?

◆ What do you like and not like about each other? Get it out into the open now!

- What do you like and dislike about each other's family?

- And, of course, what sort of wedding do you want and how much are you going to spend on it?

DECIDING WHO IS GOING TO BE TOLD FIRST

It's usual for you to tell immediate family first and then close friends, but the order is up to you. If your family is important to you, the engagement is a good time to get to know more about the background and expectations of the person you're marrying. Most people have a model of marriage in their minds that's based on their own experience. If two people with very different family experiences plan to marry, the marriage has more chance of surviving if they at least know what their partner is expecting.

HAVING A PARTY

You don't *need* to have a party – only if you want one.

Old-fashioned engagement parties

These can be fun and needn't be too lavish. The advantages are that:

- you get presents (though not usually ones you'd actually want because it's definitely not done to have an engagement list!); and

- it's a good trial run for the wedding because it gives you a chance to check out in advance who's going to behave badly and whether the families get on together in a social situation.

American-style engagement showers
These parties are currently popular. The bride has a girly tea party with her friends, who shower her with personal presents or silly household ones. Apparently, rubber gloves with fake jewels on are a current favourite.

Engagement showers can be a nice idea for brides who might feel they've neglected their girlfriends while they've been involved in the early stages of an intensive relationship with their future partner. It's also a good time to sound out girlfriends for potential bridesmaids.

PLANNING THE WEDDING WITH YOUR PARTNER
Make sure you have actually talked about the wedding and agreed:

◆ what you're going to spend;
◆ whom you want to invite; and
◆ how much you expect your families to contribute.

GETTING DISENGAGED
Sometimes, however right it seems at the time, an engagement doesn't always end in marriage. And, tough as it may sound, when that happens it is *always* a good thing. If there are any doubts on either side, it's best to find out at the engagement stage. Although an engagement isn't a legally binding contract any more, getting engaged sometimes seems to bring home to one of the couple the seriousness of what he or she is entering into. If you or your partner should change your mind at this stage, it's going to be distressing and perhaps embarrassing as well – but it's a lot better to find out now than after the wedding.

If you do get disengaged, it's good manners to give back your engagement presents. If the bride has broken the engagement, she should offer to give the ring back to the bridegroom and he can make his own decision about whether or not to accept it. If the bridegroom breaks off the engagement, the bride is theoretically entitled to keep the ring unless, of course, it's a family heirloom. If that's the case she should hand it back but might expect a piece of jewellery in return. Make sure you tell everyone personally that the wedding is off.

Never say bad things publicly about your ex-spouse-to-be. This will reflect badly on you for choosing him or her in the first place and he or she can always get his or her own back in spades.

TRICKY SITUATIONS

Situation
You suspect your boyfriend may be planning to surprise you with an engagement ring but you don't trust his judgement on jewellery.

Solution
Assuming you are going to accept the ring, you'd better start dropping hints when you pass a jeweller's shop or see a friend with an engagement ring. My daughter pasted up pictures of the ring she liked on her future fiancé's bathroom mirror and it worked. But it's not very subtle.

Situation
You want to propose romantically to your girlfriend and surprise her with a ring, but you aren't sure what sort of ring she'd like.

Solution

You can do one of three things:

◆ Sound her out in advance by talking about jewellery (not an option most men feel comfortable with).

◆ Just buy a rock – a big diamond is usually a safe choice – they go with everything.

◆ Select a single diamond and give her that instead of an actual ring. You can then take her to choose her own setting and add other stones if she wants them.

Situation

You come from very different backgrounds and the families have never met. You're worried about how they will cope with meeting each other for an engagement dinner or lunch.

Solution

The answer depends on how big the difference is:

◆ If the differences are minor, you can probably use the engagement period to make sure the two families get to know each other well enough to feel comfortable at the wedding. For the first meeting it's probably best to be on neutral ground and meet at a restaurant. Make sure it's quiet enough to talk and not so upmarket or expensive that anyone is likely to feel intimidated.

◆ If, on the other hand, the differences are more serious and one set of parents is likely to disapprove of the other, the sooner you tackle the problem the better. If there are major racial or cultural differences it may mean one or both of you accepting that this marriage means withdrawing to some degree from your own family background. Whatever you do, don't just assume that it will be alright – this kind of difference is a major factor in marriage breakup and it's best tackled up front.

Sit down together and each write a list of what you expect your perfect partner to do for you when you're married, then write a list of what you expect to do for your partner. Swap the lists and talk about them.

ENGAGEMENT CHECKLIST

☐ Choosing the ring is an important initiation ceremony. If you get one you're both happy with, that's a very good sign. If, on the other hand, you can't agree or see each other's point of view, you may want to take a look at the reasons why.

☐ The engagement is a good time to get to know more about each other's backgrounds and expectations. Make sure you are both agreed on what sort of wedding you want and how much you're prepared to spend.

☐ Remember this is one of the most positive, joyful, optimistic commitments you will ever make, and the engagement period is a time for having fun and being sociable with friends and family. If you approach it with this point of view, planning the wedding will be a pleasure not a chore.

$\bigcirc\!\!\!2$

Paying for and Planning the Wedding

Weddings are expensive, but there are lots of things you can do to keep the costs under control – not least by asking your-self what's most important to you: getting married or keeping everybody happy? However, weddings are all about creating a new family, which is a good reason to make them family occasions. Whatever type of wedding you decide on, how-ever, you should both be totally happy with it.

TRADITIONAL WEDDINGS

In the past it was simple – the bride's parents paid for everything before the wedding and the bridegroom took on the financial responsibility for his new bride afterwards.

Who paid for what

The *bridegroom* paid for:

- the engagement ring and wedding ring;

- the stag party;

- his own suit and probably the best man's and ushers' suits as well;

- flowers for the bride and bridesmaids as well as buttonholes for himself, the best man, ushers and star guests;

- civil or church ceremony fees;

- presents for the bride, bridesmaids, pages, ushers and best man;

- transport away from the reception and the wedding night venue;

- the press announcement for the wedding; and

- the honeymoon.

The bridegroom may have got off lightly at the wedding but, afterwards, he'd be expected to keep his wife in the manner to which she was accustomed. She'd give up working as soon as she was wed because being a housewife was recognised at that time as being a full-time job. And, of course, any children who came along would also be the husband's sole financial responsibility.

Hardly surprising, then, that the bride's father paid for the entire wedding as a kind of parting gesture. The cost and style of the wedding would depend partly on what he could afford and partly on the impression he wanted to make on the bridegroom's family and his social circle. The fact that her husband was paying for the wedding gave the bride's mother the right to act as hostess and organise the show, usually with some assistance from the bride.

The *bride* paid for:

◆ the hen party;

◆ the groom's ring;

◆ something old, new, borrowed and blue;

◆ the hairdresser and beautician on the day for herself and her bridesmaids;

◆ the going-away outfit; and

◆ a present for the bridegroom.

The *bride and groom* paid for a present for the bride's parents. The *best man* paid for any wedding fees payable on the day with money the bridegroom had given him in advance. The *guests* paid for the wedding presents, which they chose themselves because wedding lists were considered to be vulgar. This meant multiple toasters and, before that, toast racks. There would also be a lot of vases and other theoretically ornamental items which guests had probably been given at their own weddings and wanted to get rid of.

The *bride's parents* paid for:

- the engagement party;

- the bride's dress, bridesmaid's dress and all their accessories;

- the cake;

- flowers in church and at the reception;

- wedding cars;

- the reception venue, decorations and gifts for the guests;

- catering and drinks;

- reception entertainment;

- the bride's going-away outfit; and

- wedding insurance.

Because the bride's parents paid for most of the wedding and reception costs, they were officially the hosts and sent out the invitations. The bride's mother would play a major role in helping her daughter to plan and organise the whole show.

The bridegroom's parents had very little to do other than host the family engagement dinner and turn up on the wedding day.

WEDDINGS TODAY

The cost of a wedding today can be very high, and the bride and groom will usually pay for a large part of it themselves with voluntary contributions from both sets of parents. It's safest to assume you'll have to foot most of the bill yourselves while gratefully and gracefully accepting contributions from both sets of parents, godparents and friends of the family.

There are some special items the bride's parents might still like to pay for, and these include:

◆ the wedding dress and veil;
◆ bridesmaids' dresses; and
◆ flowers.

The bridegroom's parents, on the other hand, are more likely to offer to be responsible for a specific wedding item, such as drinks or catering, or even wedding cars.

THE COST

The average UK wedding in 2002 was costed out by weddingguideuk.com as follows:

	£
Bride's wedding ring	200
Groom's wedding ring	150
Wedding dress	700
Headdress and veil	150

Bridal bouquet	75
Shoes and accessories	125
Bride's beauty treatments	75
Bridesmaids' dresses	500
Groom's outfit	150
Flowers (buttonholes, church, etc.)	200
Printing	300
Wedding cars	300
Civil/church fees	200
Photographs	400
Video	400
Wedding cake	200
Reception venue or marquee	600
Reception decorations	150
Wedding reception	2,000
Evening reception	750
Drinks	750
Entertainment	500
Bride's going-away outfit	150
Wedding night venue	125
Honeymoon	1,500
Wedding insurance	50
Other expenses	300
Total	**11,000**

Most people are shocked when they see this total – but none of these individual expenses is over the top for a modern wedding.

Coping with the costs

There's a lot you can do to keep the costs under control. Not least is to ask yourself what's most important to you

– getting married or keeping everybody happy? Having said that, weddings are all about creating a new family, which is a good reason to make them a family occasion, and you may want to make a choice between inviting *everybody* to share beer and sandwiches at your local pub or inviting only a select few to a champagne and smoked salmon reception at a minor stately home.

Whatever your decision, be sure you are both totally happy with it. When you are, you can work out how to sell that decision to your parents and other interested parties.

Financial strategies

When you've answered the question about whom you want to be involved in your wedding, the next thing to do is to work out a **budget**. Decide how much you can realistically afford to spend. Write it down and share it with your parents and any other financial contributors.

Decide **when** you're going to get married. Once you know how long you've got to raise the money you can set up a plan for getting it together. This might include a change of lifestyle (less going out for a while) or a special savings account. Buying an extra lottery ticket every week was one bridegroom's idea of a contribution to the wedding fund but it only resulted in reducing the wedding kitty by £46 – the cost of the bridesmaids' flowers.

Start collecting **comparative costings** for *everything* and, when you have them all, you can go through the list and work out what's within your budget and what is definitely out. It may seem obvious, but lots of couples don't do this

– they choose everything separately according to what takes their fancy and then panic when they realise just how much they've committed themselves to pay.

Remember that **timing** may affect costs. Wedding venues are often cheaper in the autumn and winter than in spring and summer. Weekday weddings can also be cheaper because fewer people are able to come and so your guest list will be shorter.

Check your **suppliers**. Small, local suppliers for items such as the cake may be cheaper if they aren't VAT registered. Always get quotes *in writing* so that you can be sure of your budget totals and also so that you can make sure it doesn't suddenly escalate at the last minute. Look at each item individually and ask yourself what you can beg, borrow or do yourself. For example, you might have someone in the family who arranges flowers, makes dresses or cakes or has a car you could use on the day.

Remember that anything **handmade**, besides being much cheaper, is usually considered charming. Invitations are a case in point – if you or anyone else in the family is prepared to invest some time, it's not difficult to make your own invitations at the cost of some fancy card and ribbon. If you don't happen to know a calligrapher you can always have a very simple printed insert and dress it up. Flowers and venue decorations are another potential DIY item, provided you can muster enough willing helpers the night before the wedding.

Going for the **cheaper option** can be presented as a *style* rather than a budget decision. Just recently a number of *Hello*-style weddings have featured sausages and mash washed down with beer at some otherwise glitzy wedding receptions. Having a late afternoon ceremony followed immediately by the reception can save having to provide both a lunch and an evening party.

INSURANCE

Insurance may sound a bit pessimistic but, with the current costs of weddings, it makes a lot of sense. The cost of insuring a wedding varies from about £40 to £200 depending on the amount insured. It will cover you not only for cancellation but also for public liability (if someone is injured at the reception), damage to wedding clothes, loss of rings, disappearance of the cake and even professional counselling should either of you be left at the altar.

THE WEDDING LIST

Nowadays it's taken for granted that there will be a wedding list, and most people happily send it out with the invitations without feeling embarrassed. If you do happen to feel a bit shy about this, just think how much more delicate it is than the situation in certain eastern traditions where a price tag is actually attached to the wedding invitation. If you accept, you pay for your ticket, which is calculated to cover the cost of the reception, plus a margin for the bride and groom.

There are two ways of doing the list.

Simple checklists

You can draw up a simple checklist of all the things you

need, including precise details about design, manufacturer and price. The problem with this is that one of you has to take responsibility for keeping track of who has bought what. If you simply hand out the list there's nothing to stop everyone from buying you teaspoons while leaving you without any knives and forks. Having to take calls from your family and friends about what they want to buy for you can be time consuming and embarrassing, especially when you get to the stage where all the cheaper items have already been bought.

A list placed with a particular shop

You can have more than one of these and a very wide range of retailers (from Argos to Harrods) how offer this service. The great thing about this way of doing it is that your guests don't actually have to go shopping and they don't even have to see the list! They can simply phone the shop, ask for a price range and then pick whereabouts on that price range they want their present to be. The shop then gives them a couple of choices – a casserole dish or wine glasses, perhaps. The guest selects the one he or she wants and reads out his or her credit card details. The shop will then wrap and deliver the present on behalf of the guest. This service is also available on the Internet.

Some guests will always want to choose, wrap and deliver their gift personally and, if that happens, you have no alternative but to be delighted with whatever you get.

Whether or not you put your wedding presents on display is up to you. This was traditionally done at the reception or at the bride's home, with each item labelled as to whom it was from and a separate list of people who had given cheques (but not detailing the amount). Today this kind of display is generally the exception rather than the rule.

Whatever you do and whatever you get, remember to keep a list, preferably with a duplicate, of all the presents you receive and the names of the people who gave them. If you don't, you won't be able to write your thank-you letters and, although that might sound quite appealing right now, it's probably not worth the guilt and embarrassment you'll probably feel afterwards.

WHOM TO INVITE

The number of people you invite is obviously one of the biggest factors in determining the cost of your wedding. The hardest choice is usually between friends, family and, if your career is important to you, your colleagues. Here are some factors you might want to take into account:

♦ Make a list of the people you really care about – the ones you see, or at least talk to, on a daily or weekly basis.

♦ Add to the list the people who have been important to you in the past – people who played a part in your life when you were younger.

♦ What about the people you work with every day? Do you count them all as friends or are you thinking of inviting them because it's 'expected'?

♦ Then there are the people who are contributing towards the cost of the wedding. They may feel they are entitled to have a say in whom you invite.

- If you and your partner have families of different sizes, does the one with the smaller family feel entitled to ask some more distant relatives just to even up the guest list?

- Do you mostly share mutual friends or are you both still a part of separate social groups?

- Who will you need to support you in the future as you move into a different phase of your life as part of a pair?

This list can help you sort out your guest list, with due regard to both economics and emotions. This is what you do. You both need to read through these points and, when you've given each one due consideration, you'll find it much easier to make separate personal lists of the people who really matter. Get together and compare your lists. Talk through your differences.

If you're still faced with too many people and too little money or too little space, you can give yourselves a trial run in matrimonial decision-making:

- Do you hire a larger but cheaper venue?

- Do you go for a cheaper catering option?

- Do you restrict the guest list mostly to family or mostly to friends?

- Who will be offended and why does it matter?

- Are you going to insist that each of you invites the same number of people?

◆ Are you tempted to give up and get married abroad –
just the two of you?

This is always an interesting exercise because it's based on
your values about people. It doesn't matter what your
values are, but if you share them with your prospective
partner you will find it relatively easy to sort out your
guest list together.

TRICKY SITUATIONS

Situation
Your bride-to-be has wealthy parents but she hasn't asked
them for a wedding contribution and they haven't offered.

Solution
This isn't a money issue, it's about communication. Why
haven't they offered and why hasn't she asked? You need
the answers to these two questions before you get married
because it sounds as though there's a problem in there
somewhere and it might be a hereditary one. Open up the
dialogue and find out as quickly as you can.

Situation
Your stepfather has offered to pay most of the wedding
expenses and can afford to do it. You're not surprised
because he's always treated you like his own daughter and
you get on well with him. But your natural father has also
said he'd like to pay, although you know he'd need to take
out a bank loan to do it. Can you take advantage of your
stepfather's generous offer without offending your birth
father?

Solution

Here are your options:

- Take your stepfather into your confidence to see if he will do it anonymously. If he gave you the money rather than paying the bills directly you could tell your natural father that you and your bridegroom are paying for everything and that you can easily afford to do so.

- Talk to your natural father and tell him that you would value his involvement in the wedding far more than a contribution towards the costs. Is there anything he can do practically which would help? Is he going to give you a lot of support on the day and be nice to your mother at the reception?

- You could avoid offending anybody by resigning yourself to paying for everything personally.

Situation

You have been living together for a while and you have everything you need. Can you put cash instead of toasters on your wedding list?

Solution

You can put a discreet little note in with the invitation saying that cheques are welcome but you can't insist on it:

- The best way is not to send out a list but to put out the word informally through as many friends and relatives as possible that you don't need another cheese grater but that a cheque would be fine.

♦ Alternatively, you can put some large items on a list – things like fridges and freezers and even the honeymoon – with a note saying that contributions are welcome. You can even set up a special bank account for the purpose.

Situation

Is it rude to ask bridesmaids to contribute to the cost of their dresses and buy their own shoes?

Solution

In theory this is acceptable, but in practice, when you are choosing what they should wear, you really ought to pay for it as well. You could always set a budget and tell them what it is. Then explain that they can help choose a dress they really like but that you can only pay up to the sum on your budget.

Situation

Your fiancé has hundreds of relatives and they all expect to be invited to the wedding. Since your parents are paying, you feel it's a bit unfair that his side of the family outnumbers yours.

Solution

Ask yourself whether anybody you care about is actually being excluded because of his excessively large family and, if that's the case, you are justified in protesting. But if all your nearest and dearest are already invited and it's just a numbers game, could you just be feeling a little insecure? Talk it through with him and share your doubts. He may have put all his relatives on the list simply because his parents expect him to and he hasn't bothered to question it. You could agree to restrict the guest list to closer friends and family on both sides and perhaps go for a more glamorous venue, or stick with inviting everyone to a more modest celebration.

Situation

The wedding venue you've chosen can only accommodate a limited number of people, which means you can just about squeeze in your closest family and your very best friends. But your father, who is paying for the whole thing, wants to invite some long-standing friends of the family which would mean striking some of your own close friends off the list. Can you insist your own friends have priority?

Solution

Explain that your overflowing guest list means you will have to economise on the venue and catering. Hopefully, this will either inspire your father to put in more funds in order to maintain standards or see your point of view and give you priority over his golfing buddies.

> *Until you've got a good relationship with yourself, you are not going to make a good relationship with someone else.*

WEDDING BUDGET CHECKLIST

☐ Find out whether you are likely to get any financial help from your parents or any other sources.

☐ Once you have an overall budget, make a comprehensive list of every possible expense (see Chapter 11).

☐ Allocate the budget between the different items, allowing £500 for the unexpected. The chances are that you will have overspent already – on paper at least.

☐ Agree with your future partner about how you will cope with the overspend. Go through the items again and work out where you can compromise or cut back. Factor in any non-financial support you may get from family and friends in terms of cake making, flower arranging, providing cars, creating wedding stationery or any other service they might be able to offer.

☐ Set a final budget for your wedding and agree to stick to it.

The Bride and Groom: Roles and Responsibilities

If you're reading this book because you're the bride or the bridegroom, you don't need reminding that you are the most important people in this wedding. The trouble is that brides and bridegrooms often spend so much time on the wedding arrangements and keeping other people happy that they sometimes forget about keeping close to each other and having fun together.

TRADITIONAL ROLES

There is traditionally a complete separation of the bride and groom's respective roles in the period leading up to the wedding. In the past, the bride and groom often saw less of each other immediately before the wedding because each were involved in separate preparations for the big day. The bridegroom would be celebrating the end of his bachelorhood with his friends, organising the honeymoon and making sure his employers and colleagues could manage without him for a week or so. The bride, on the other hand, would be frantically rushing around trying to complete all the final preparations for herself and the reception.

Of course, bride and groom would not, traditionally, have been living together, and even if a bride was living independently she would return to her parents' house shortly before the wedding.

Lucky brides

Almost all the traditional wedding superstitions are to do with the bride rather than the groom.

Something old, something new, something borrowed and something blue: everybody knows this one, and most brides can manage all four. The wedding dress is usually something new, something old can be a piece of family jewellery, something blue is often a garter (traditionally a gift from the chief bridesmaid) and something borrowed can be anything from a bottle of your bridesmaid's nail varnish to your granny's handkerchief.

And there are plenty of other good omens for the day:

◆ Being woken up by birdsong.

◆ Stepping out of the house to the church right foot first.

◆ A sprig of lavender in the wedding bouquet means a long and happy marriage.

◆ Seeing a black cat, a chimney sweep, a lamb, a dove or a toad on the way to church.

◆ Finding a spider in your wedding dress.

◆ Wearing an old veil that has been worn by a happily married woman.

◆ Sunshine brings happiness, but every drop of rain is a blessing, especially if you're getting married in Ireland.

Lucky bridegrooms
Superstitions about the bridegroom seem to be more about avoiding bad luck than having good luck. It's bad luck for him if he:

◆ sees the wedding dress before the wedding or if he sees the bride before the ceremony on the day of the wedding;

◆ drops the ring before putting it on the bride's finger – that means he will be ruled by her in the future;

◆ turns back for anything after leaving for the church; or

◆ pays for the ceremony himself – he should do it through the best man.

And, at last, a good one – carrying the bride over the threshold of their home after the wedding will bring good fortune to them both.

ROLES TODAY

The bride and groom are more likely to be working together on the wedding preparations, which means they'll still be seeing each other although they may not be spending much time together. But even if a couple have been living together for years, a bride may still want to be married from her parents' house – or stay in the same hotel as her parents the night before the wedding.

And there are still some completely separate items on the 'to do' lists of the bride and groom.

THE BRIDE'S LIST

Wedding dress and accessories

The sooner you start shopping for your wedding dress the better. You'll have time to find exactly what you want and either save up for it or have it made to fit. You'll also have more chance of finding a bargain in a sale (usually January and midsummer). Wedding-dress shopping is a lengthy process: you will usually need to make an appointment and allow at least two hours. Each of the shops will specialise in just a few designers so, to get a good idea of the range that's available, you have to be prepared to visit quite a few of them. It takes stamina and determination and, after a while, they all start to look the same.

This is a major expenditure. A dress can cost between £250 and £5,000, but don't assume the more expensive ones will necessarily suit you better. A very upmarket bride recently walked down the aisle in a £200 Monsoon dress with a million pounds worth of jewellery round her neck and in her hair. She'd probably have looked just as good without the jewellery.

The following are some points you might want to bear in mind when choosing your wedding dress and accessories:

♦ Think back to a time when you had an evening dress that really suited you. What was it about that particular dress that made it look so good?

♦ Ask yourself what look you want to achieve and then bear it in mind when you're trying on your dresses. Is it glamour? Innocence? Sophistication? Sex appeal? Do you want to be Grace Kelly? Audrey Hepburn? Marilyn Monroe? Madonna? Ru Paul?

♦ Always take somebody with you – two people are even better because you get more than one opinion and they can talk among themselves while you're being pinned into yet another long white frock.

♦ It's considered bad luck to try on the entire wedding outfit before the actual wedding day, so you can always keep the shoes separate until the last minute and just wear a pair with the same heel height. It's very important to see the dress with the headdress, veil, gloves, wrap, jewellery and even a mock bouquet to find out whether the whole look is going to work.

- When you're trying on dresses wear a strapless bra and pale tights. It's hard to make a decision if you've got a blue bra strap hanging out at the top and black tights showing at the bottom.

- On the wedding day, plan your underwear both before and after you put the dress on. I once saw a bride walk up the aisle in a backless dress with the red mark from the bra she'd just taken off clearly visible to the whole congregation. If you've any doubts, don't wear a bra at all until you get into the dress.

- When it comes to wedding jewellery, less is usually more, especially if you're wearing a very glittery headpiece. Remember to switch your engagement ring from your left hand to your right hand before you leave for the ceremony. Try this out in advance and, if it's too small to fit on your right hand, you may have to leave it at home or ask someone to look after it until you get to the reception.

- If you are getting married in a religious setting, bear in mind that some churches and temples will not allow bare shoulders or even bare arms. Find this out first.

- Another reason for covering up is the weather. If you're having a winter wedding give some thought to how you will keep warm as you go from your car to the ceremony and the ceremony to the reception. Some big churches are pretty chilly too.

- Make sure it's actually wearable – wedding receptions are getting longer and more elaborate so it's not unusual to be wearing your wedding outfit (and dancing in it too) for 12 hours or more. Wear the shoes at home in the pre-wedding week and don't go for very high heels if you don't normally wear them – you'll look like a drag queen.

◆ The most important thing to remember about choosing a wedding dress is to allow time after each shopping session to have a drink and something to eat with your supporting team. This whole process is fun, it's not a chore. So enjoy it.

Bridesmaid's dresses and accessories
Once you've chosen your own dress you'll have a much better idea of what sort of bridesmaids dresses you want:

◆ They should complement yours – you should look like you're dancing in the same troupe.

◆ They should also look terrific on your bridesmaids. If a bridesmaid doesn't look good in her dress it doesn't make you look better; on the contrary, it reflects badly on you as well. They shouldn't outshine you, but they should look lovely. If they don't, they'll be unhappy and grouchy, embarrassed bridesmaids don't do anything for the atmosphere or the photos.

◆ Try to pick your bridesmaids so that they look reasonably good together. This isn't always possible when friendships and family obligations are involved, but putting your fat friend on parade in a tight dress with three of your thin friends is just unkind.

◆ If you have one bridesmaid who's more difficult to dress than the others, find a couple of styles and colours that will suit her first and then try them on the others.

♦ Ask them what they want and tell them to be honest about what they hate in terms of styles and colours.

♦ Make sure they'll be warm enough. You may be prepared to freeze on your big day, but there's no reason why they should have to. Wedding wraps are disproportionately expensive but you could have some simple cloaks made out of glamorous material with perhaps a fake fur trim.

♦ Don't worry about it being something they can wear afterwards – if they go to a lot of balls or cocktail parties then perhaps they will. But wedding outfits were never meant to be practical. I went to a wedding recently where the bride's mother had decreed that the bridesmaids wore Laura Ashley summer dresses so that they would get the wear out of them afterwards. They looked like a team of librarians.

Your bridesmaids are normally your sisters or best friends. If you want a bridesmaid who is married or pregnant, she becomes a matron of honour. Small children (who are usually a lot of trouble but look good in the photos) are pages and flower girls. If you have trouble choosing who your attendants should be, ask yourself the following questions:

♦ Is there somebody I need to involve in the wedding – maybe someone from the bridegroom's family?

- Is this person going to be supportive and helpful and fun?

- Is this person going to look good following me up the aisle?

Hair, make-up and other beauty treatments
This is a time to pamper yourself. You want to feel good and look good on the day – you'll never have as many photos taken in your life (unless you're a media person) as you will when you get married:

- Start several months before the wedding with body and mind workouts. Get yourself fit and join a gym – that extra level of fitness will come in handy when you're running around in the last few weeks putting all the arrangements together!

- Don't neglect your mental state – this is a good time to practise relaxation techniques, deep breathing and taking a bit of time every day to think about what you want out of life. This is a big step you're taking, so be aware of what you want out of marriage and what you're prepared to put into it.

- Get into a good routine of skin cleansing and moisturising and don't forget the body lotion *every* time you have a shower.

- Experiment with your hair. If you're not confident about your hairdresser, try a few different ones. There are some that specialise in bridal hairstyles (see Chapter 12). Bear in mind weather conditions and, if you're going for a completely different look or colour, try it out a couple of months before the wedding.

- Unless you're a make-up expert and used to changing your look on a regular basis, go for a make-up lesson or two. Always wear white and have your hair done in something like your wedding day style so that you know which bits of your face are most exposed. Wear your wedding make-up in public and under all kinds of lighting before the day and, if you're hiring a make-up artist, get to know him or her and give him or her two or three trial runs. Get any plucking, waxing and facials done in advance to give the redness time to settle down.

- Wedding make-up needs staying power: you will be kissed, hugged, cried over and probably rained on if it's an English wedding. Use waterproof mascara and give your bridesmaids a full make-up kit, hairbrush, spray and pins in case you need repairs.

- Get a manicure, even if you would normally varnish your own nails. Professional manicures last longer and your hands are going to be photographed when you're showing off your ring, cutting the cake and throwing your bouquet.

- You might consider including your bridesmaids and perhaps both the mothers as well in some of these hair and make-up experiments (see hen parties in Chapter 5).

Presents for the bridesmaids

In theory these are the bridegroom's job but they are usually glad to hand it over to the bride. It's traditionally jewellery – though it doesn't have to be. Little heart-shaped dressing-table boxes or picture frames are nice. And silver is great because it's precious but relatively inexpensive. Think about what they'd really like rather than what the wedding catalogues suggest.

Present for the groom

You don't have to give your bridegroom a present, but it is traditional. It's usually jewellery (which, for men, used to mean cufflinks or nothing) and you should know him well enough to know what he'd like. If you opt for cufflinks, having simple gold or silver ones engraved with your names and the date of the wedding is much more personal than wedding catalogue ones with 'bridegroom' stamped on them. You can also have jewellery made to your own design and it's not as expensive as you might think. Check out some small local jewellers until you find a creative one.

Presents for the mothers

Often a bunch of flowers, presented at the reception is all it takes. But a silver photo frame, perhaps with the wedding date on it, is perfect. Although the bride's mother is likely to have worked the hardest, they have to be treated equally.

Presents for the grandmothers

This isn't obligatory, but if there are any very elderly grannies at the reception it's a very nice touch to give them a bouquet – or at least a special mention in one of the speeches and a round of applause.

Co-ordinating everyone

Make sure your mother and mother-in-law are talking to each other as well as to you about what they are wearing. Clashing outfits or, worse still, identical ones, could be a disaster. It will look a lot better on the day if they are wearing something that tones in with your general colour scheme, so don't leave it to chance.

Remember that, in theory, everyone is there to give you help and support. Your mother and your bridesmaids, in particular, should be taking some of the strain. In practice, of course, modern brides usually do most of it themselves, but do you really have to? Step back, take a deep breath and ask for help. People love getting involved in wedding preparations, and whether it's making table decorations or coming with you on shopping trips they'll probably be happy to volunteer.

THE BRIDEGROOM'S LIST

When asked what she thought the bridegroom's responsibilities were, one bride answered sharply, 'whatever I tell him!' Most things, apart from choosing the bride's dress, can be shared – and they often are. Twenty-first century bridegrooms have been known to help with everything from icing the cake to hemming the bridesmaids dresses but, if you are the bridegroom, you should know that there are still a few things that are considered to be your primary responsibility.

Choosing your best man and ushers

Often the bride will want some of her own family to share the ushering duties but it's your responsibility as bridegroom to make sure they are briefed and organised for the day. The best man, on the other hand, is there for you – so it's your choice. And it's also your fault if he gets drunk at the reception and gives the sort of speech that makes the bride wish she'd never married you. You could always opt for a best man team and have two or three best men. That way, if one of them falls down on the job at least you'll have a backup.

Shopping for a gift for the best man, a gift for the bride and a wedding ring

If you can't think of anything to buy your best man and you don't want to give the traditional cufflinks, buy him something you'd like yourself.

The wedding gift for the bride has to be a surprise – usually sent round to her on the morning of the wedding before the ceremony. It could be earrings or a necklace – but only if she's dropped some hints about what would go with her dress. A bracelet could be safer – but if you're not absolutely sure, ask her mother or the chief bridesmaid.

You give your bride the ring on her wedding day. But the chances are you'll have chosen it together so that it will go with the engagement ring and with your own wedding ring if you're going to wear one.

Booking the honeymoon

You might like to make this a surprise for the bride and not tell her until the very last minute that you're taking her bird-watching in Newfoundland. But, even if she has some choice in the matter, it should be your job to make all the arrangements. Don't forget to check that you both have any necessary vaccinations well before the wedding – a red lump on the bride's arm is unattractive. Find out, too, if she's taking your name and wants to travel with her new passport.

Writing a speech for the reception
Don't panic – read Chapter 9.

Choosing what you, the ushers and best men are going to wear
This can also involve other members of the bridal party, such as the fathers of the bride and groom and other close relatives. It's no good insisting on everyone wearing morning suits with damask waistcoats if most of the men are going to feel embarrassed in them or if some of them are overweight. They will look as though they are in fancy dress. So before you head down to Moss Bros to see if you can get a discount on a dozen top hats, stop to think what you're all going to look like.

Talk to the bride and see what kind of suits will go best with her dress and the bridesmaids' dresses. If she's insisting on a morning suit and you know you'll look silly, get her to come along with you, just for the laugh, when you try it on.

When you've made a decision, book the suit-hire company in plenty of time – wedding outfitters get very busy in summer. And if you decide to buy yourself a suit or have it made, allow plenty of time for that too.

Getting yourself in shape
Most brides make the effort of their lives to look beautiful on their wedding day and it's up to you to return the complement by taking a bit of trouble yourself. This used to mean a haircut and a new suit but standards are higher now. At least six months before the day, take a look in the mirror and ask yourself if now would be a good time to

take a bit more exercise, drink a bit more water and adopt that healthier lifestyle you've been thinking about.

TRICKY SITUATIONS

Situation
You can't afford to spend £500 or more on a dress but you haven't seen anything you like for less than that.

Solution
Here are the possibilities:

◆ Think about a second-hand dress – newspaper ads, charity shops and even dry cleaners are worth checking.

◆ Find the style you want and see if you can get a local dressmaker (not a couturier) to copy it for you.

◆ Look in the budget shops like Monsoon – you might find something that is just perfect for you.

◆ Find out when all the wedding dress designers sell their sample dresses. They will need cleaning, but if you're a size 12 to 14 you might get a real bargain.

◆ Check the wedding dress sales (usually January and October).

◆ Think about buying a very simple, plain cream or ivory evening gown and adding some lace and a jacket to turn it into a wedding dress.

Situation

Your fiancé won't take an interest in the wedding and is leaving everything to you.

Solution

This is always a sign that there's some communicating to be done. Does he really want to get married? Does he want a completely different wedding style from the one you're planning? Or is it just that he can't see a role for himself in the whirlwind of activity you've created? Find out which it is and sort it out.

Find out what really matters to your partner. The more personal values you share now, the more years of marriage you're likely to share in future.

BRIDE AND GROOM'S CHECKLIST

☐ Always remember why you're getting married – the reason(s) vary from one couple to another, but now is a good time to make a list of your personal ones. In fact, you should both make a list and then compare them. Hopefully you'll share at least one of the reasons.

☐ Take time out to check that your future spouse is happy with all the arrangements.

☐ Take time out to relax and have fun together.

☐ Be ready to indulge yourself and other people.

☐ Remember that this is the best time ever to forgive and forget old quarrels and to discard old hang-ups you no longer need.

☐ Write everything down on your 'to do' list and make sure you get it all done well ahead of time. During the week before the wedding you owe it to yourself and your partner to be in the best possible shape.

☐ Aim to enjoy the preparations and spend some quality time with people you love.

4

The Wedding Team: Roles and Responsibilities

However well organised you are, if you want to be relaxed enough on the day to enjoy your wedding, you're going to have to depend on other people. Therefore you need to make a list of everything you're going to need help with, before, during and after the wedding.

TRADITIONAL ROLES

In the past, weddings were complex social arrangements. The bridal couple played a much smaller role than they do today and their parents, best man, ushers, bridesmaids and other attendants had clearly defined and very important duties to perform.

The best man, for example, was chosen not for his ability to make speeches but because of his strength and courage. He was supposed to assist his friend in capturing a bride and stay with the couple until the wedding was performed in case a rival tried to claim her or her family wanted her back. Even the ushers were expected to keep potential troublemakers from getting into the church. The best man and ushers in mediaeval times were a team of bouncers and thugs and, although they were usually friends of the groom, they could also be hired mercenaries.

The bridesmaids, on the other hand, were there to chaperone the bride night and day to make sure she didn't entertain any male visitors before her wedding. They were also expected to work hard at making her look as beautiful as possible so that the bridegroom didn't change his mind at the altar. The less of a dowry she had, the more important her appearance would be.

ROLES TODAY

Apart from the bride and groom who, by law, must be female and male respectively, most of the other important wedding roles can now be taken by either males or females, some more readily than others. It's not unusual to have female best men and ushers, brides can be given away by other women and fathers can organise weddings. It's more unusual to have male bridesmaids but this has been done in a recent, much publicised TV wedding.

THE BEST MAN

So the modern best man doesn't have to be a man. And he or she isn't expected to fight for the bridegroom, which is just as well because they'd be far too busy. Apart from the bride's mother, the best man, in theory at least, has more to do than anyone else on the wedding day. In practice, a lot of the duties on his list are shared out among different members of the wedding party.

But, because the best man's job is potentially so pivotal, it's vitally important that he discusses it with the groom (and probably the bride as well) and finds out well in advance exactly what he is going to be responsible for and which tasks will be taken over by someone else.

Best man's job description

The following are the best man's main jobs. To:

- talk through the wedding plans in detail with the groom and probably the bride as well;

- help choose the ushers and to take responsibility for briefing and organising them;

- protect and look after the bridegroom at the stag night;

- get the bridegroom's outfits, his own outfit and the outfits for the ushers organised and to collect them before the wedding, and to make sure all the bits (hats, gloves, waistcoats, etc.) are all there; and

◆ prepare his speech (see Chapter 9). If there's a best man team he could share the speech, which sometimes makes it a bit less scary – or, alternatively, they could all make one!

Before the wedding

Before the wedding the best man is theoretically responsible for just about everything that involves the bridegroom. He needs to get together with the groom a least a couple of hours before the wedding to make sure he's sober and correctly dressed. He should also do the following:

◆ Check that the groom has everything he needs for the honeymoon, including luggage, tickets and passports.

◆ Take charge of the wedding rings and any fees that need to be paid on the day.

◆ Take the groom to the wedding venue at least half an hour before it's due to start and call the bride's father to tell him the groom has arrived.

◆ Make sure that he, the bridegroom and the ushers all have buttonholes. If they are not being left at the wedding venue, he may have to pick them up before he goes to collect the bridegroom. The flower should be pointing up not down, with the pin behind the lapel.

◆ Check that the ushers know what they are doing and that everybody is in the right place. If it's a church wedding this will have been rehearsed. If it's a civil wedding, there will be someone from the venue as well as the registrar to keep everybody on the right track.

Whatever the venue, it's likely that the best man will be standing with the bridegroom at the front of the room waiting for the bride and her father to walk in from the back. When he gets the signal from one of the ushers that the bride has arrived, he should:

◆ Stand up with the bridegroom, to his left.

◆ Hand over the rings when they are needed.

◆ Escort the chief bridesmaid or matron of honour to sign the register if they are to be the witnesses. If not, he simply waits with everyone else while the register is signed.

◆ Follow the bride and groom and their parents out of the wedding, with the chief bridesmaid on his left arm.

After the wedding

After the wedding, the best man needs to liase with the photographer, making sure he or she gets all the shots he or she needs and that the guests don't wander off until all the photos are done. His other tasks are to:

◆ find the wedding car and ask the chauffeur to be ready if the wedding ceremony and reception are being held at different venues; and

◆ make sure that all the guests have directions and transport to the reception and arrange car shares if necessary. The best man leaves just ahead of the other guests, following the bride and groom and taking the bridesmaids with him.

At the reception

At the reception, the best man joins the receiving line if invited by the bride's parents or the bride and groom. After that, he needs to establish a collection point for any wedding presents that guests have brought with them and make sure it is secure.

The best man organises the wedding meal if there isn't a toastmaster. This could include the following jobs:

◆ Inviting the priest to say grace before the meal.

◆ Reminding the guests to use the disposable cameras on the tables: are they being used right from the very beginning? It's especially important to have plenty of photos at the beginning of the evening when the decorations and flower arrangements (and the guests) are still looking their best.

◆ Watching the wine service and seeing that there is plenty of water as well as soft drinks on each table. It's important that everyone has something in their glasses for the toasts at the end.

◆ Calling silence for the speeches at the end of the meal.

◆ Asking the bride's father to speak first and then the bridegroom, who will toast the bridesmaids

◆ Finding out before the meal if there will be any extra speeches. Sometimes the bride decides to speak for herself, and the bridesmaids may want to say something on their own behalf as well. If anyone who isn't in the immediate wedding party wants to make a speech, check with the bride and groom before programming them in – weddings often bring the emotional saboteurs out of the family closets.

♦ Making his own speech – usually the last one, but there's no hard-and-fast rule. He speaks on behalf of the bridesmaids if they haven't replied for themselves and reads out messages from absent guests, finishing with a toast to the bride and groom and announcing the cutting of the cake.

After the meal

After the meal, the best man still needs to keep an eye on everything, making sure it's all going to plan:

♦ Check that the cake knife is ready at the right time and that the waiters are on hand to take it away and cut up the rest of the cake.

♦ Ask the chief bridesmaid to join him for the first dance, joining in after the bride and groom.

♦ Make sure the going-away car (if there is one) is decorated in the best possible taste and that nothing has been done that might make it unsafe to drive. At my own wedding somebody (who hasn't owned up yet) put stones in the brake cylinders and the brakes failed on the way to the honeymoon.

The best man should hang in right to the end to make sure that:

♦ everybody who wants to go home has transport and can find his or her way;

♦ everybody who's staying has a bedroom;

- nobody leaves anything behind;

- the disposable cameras are gathered up; and

- all the wedding presents are collected together and stored in a safe place.

It is also the best man's responsibility to see whose job it is to return any outfits that have been hired – the bride or groom's mother will probably do this, but it's worth checking.

USHERS

The role of the usher is undervalued. It's often given to potentially troublesome male relatives in they hope they won't get bored and disruptive, and consequently they aren't always properly briefed (another one of the best man's seemingly endless responsibilities). In fact, the ushers can be incredibly useful and it's worth making sure there are enough of them. They can do all the jobs the best man can't possibly do if he's focusing all his attention on the bridegroom.

Ushers' job description

The following are the ushers' main jobs. To:

- arrive at the wedding venue before even the groom and the best man to hand out any service sheets and to make sure that everything is in place and correctly set up;

- wait outside (at least one of the ushers should do this) to direct people who might otherwise get lost to give advice about car parking and toilets and to tell the guests to hang on to their wedding presents until the reception.

- make sure everybody sits in the right place – if it matters (see Chapter 6);

- inform the bridegroom, organist and choir when the bride is arriving;

- stay at the back throughout the ceremony to direct any late-arriving guests. In some places it's also a tradition that the ushers slip out during the service and tie ribbons on to all the guests cars so that the whole wedding party looks festive when they leave for the reception;

- co-ordinate the photographer and the guests to be photographed after the reception;

- check that the wedding car is ready;

- see that everybody knows the way to the reception and to look around to see that nothing's been left behind;

- head for the reception (again at least one of the ushers needs to be the advance party) as soon as he or she is through with photographs to check that the welcome drinks and other arrangements are in place. One or more should remain behind at the wedding ceremony until the last guest has left to check for any belongings – or even lost guests who may have been left behind;

- support the best man at the reception by circulating among the guests, making sure everyone has a drink and someone to talk to;

- direct guests to cloakrooms and bathrooms at the reception;

- collect and organise wedding presents;

- remind people to use disposable cameras and to collect them at the end of the evening; and

- help the best man check the reception venue at the end of the evening to see that nothing's been forgotten and that all the presents have been collected up.

BRIDESMAIDS

Like the best man, the bridesmaids may have a purely nominal role or a totally crucial one. The bride needs to think this through in advance and tell them what she wants them to do at the very beginning. I can recall a very stressful situation where the bride expected help with her hair, make-up and table decorations plus lots of emotional support while her bridesmaid assumed that all she needed to do was turn up on the morning looking beautiful.

The bride can have as many bridesmaids, flower girls, pages and matrons of honour (married bridesmaids) as she likes. The more there are, the more expensive it's likely to be because even if they contribute towards their own dresses, in reality the bride will pay for most of their outfits and accessories. It's a good idea to stick to just a couple of very small children (pageboys and flower girls) because they aren't always easy to keep under control and often get bored during the ceremony. However cute they look, two-year-olds having temper tantrums can be very distracting in the middle of the wedding vows. If small children are involved, it's a good idea to have their parents on hand to deal with any problems.

Chief bridesmaids' job description

The chief bridesmaid or matron of honour takes responsibility for looking after the younger bridesmaids and particularly the pages and flower girls. She will also be expected to:

◆ help the bride to choose her own dress as well as dresses for the bridesmaids and also all the shoes and accessories. A good bridesmaid gives honest feedback about the bride's choice of colour schemes and doesn't agree to wear anything that doesn't suit her. A bridesmaid who's wearing something she hates just to please the bride will look terrible in it because her feelings will show in her face. This can mean long hours of shopping and requires stamina. It's not a job to be taken lightly;

◆ supervise and support the bride on her hen night;

◆ (if required) help with flowers and venue decorations;

◆ look after the bride on the morning of the wedding. She should make sure she has some breakfast, get her to the hairdresser and make-up artist on time and get her dressed. All the bridesmaids should make sure they are completely ready at least half an hour before the bride so that they can give her their full attention while she waits to be taken to the wedding;

◆ chase up the bouquets;

◆ give the bride a final checkover just before the ceremony. The chief bridesmaid needs to carry a mirror and a basic make-up repair kit as well as tissues and safety pins;

- follow the bride up the aisle or into the room where the wedding is going to take place;

- take the bride's flowers and any other bits and pieces she may be carrying and to lift her veil;

- sign the register if she is one of the witnesses, otherwise she should sit behind the bride until the end of the wedding;

- (after the wedding) give the bride another quick once over and see if there's anything she needs before handing her flowers back in time for the photographs; and

- join the receiving line if invited and help to hostess the reception, mingling with the guests and making sure that everyone is enjoying themselves.

WITNESSES AND READERS

Sometimes, the bride and groom will ask other family members or friends to be their witnesses, rather than assuming the chief bridesmaid and best man will do it. They may also ask other people to read poems or inspirational pieces. These are ways of involving other people who are important to them.

THE BRIDE'S MOTHER

Since the bride's parents used to pay for and host the whole event, the bride's mother was, in theory at least, responsible for everything except the bridegroom and the honeymoon. In practice, it's likely that the bride and groom are paying for a lot of it themselves and they will decide how much of a role both sets of parents will play in the proceedings.

Bride's mother's job description

The bride's mother either used to do or organise every little detail of her daughter's wedding. But now she's more likely to share a lot of the tasks with her daughter and the only thing she must be absolutely sure to do is look as glamorous as possible on the day. The old saying that every bride will look like their mother in 20 year's time puts an enormous amount of pressure on them both. The following is the basic list of things the bride's mother is still most likely to take responsibility for. To:

◆ draw up the guest list with the help of bride and groom;

◆ send out the invitations (see Chapter 9);

◆ make a list of the people who accept and to draw up a seating plan with the bride;

◆ make accommodation arrangements for long-distance guests;

◆ liaise with the best man and ushers about the display of gifts if the bride wants to have them on show;

◆ organise the receiving line for guests at the reception and to hostess the reception once everyone has arrived;

◆ take the presents away from the reception and keep them until after the honeymoon;

◆ make sure that all the hired clothes are returned;

◆ have the wedding dress cleaned and stored;

◆ send out pieces of cake to guests who weren't able to come to the wedding;

- organise the photographs and take orders from the guests; and

- help the bride put together the wedding album.

THE BRIDE'S FATHER

Apart from writing cheques, the bride's father has a largely ceremonial role:

- He wears what he's told and turns up to escort his daughter to the wedding in plenty of time.

- If she's having a traditional church wedding he takes her up the aisle on his right arm and gives her right hand to the priest at the appropriate point in the service.

- He escorts the bridegroom's mother to the reception.

- Together with his wife and the bride and groom he greets the guests.

- If there is no priest to say grace, he will introduce the wedding breakfast and welcome the guests to share it.

- And, finally, when the best man introduces him, he makes a speech and proposes a toast to the bride and groom.

There are lots of other things he can do if the bride wants him to and he's willing to help, but those are the absolute basics.

BRIDEGROOM'S PARENTS

The role of the bridegroom's parents is proportionate to their financial contribution. If they are paying a substantial chunk of the costs it's likely they will play a major role in hosting the celebration, although they don't usually get involved at the pre-planning stage.

The bridegroom's mother usually takes some responsibility for rounding up and organising his side of the family and making sure they all have transport and accommodation if they need it.

TRICKY SITUATIONS

Situation

You've planned a themed wedding – can you tell your guests what you want them to wear?

Solution

Yes, you can make it clear on the invitation that they are expected to come dressed as characters from *Lord of the Rings* if that's really what you want. However, if they still turn up in morning dress and top hat there's absolutely nothing you can do. The bride and groom's parents are usually included in the discussion about what to wear, and the two mothers shouldn't take much persuading to talk to each other about clothes.

Situation

You have, at different times, promised the job of best man to your best school friend and your closest work colleague. To make matters worse, your twin brothers also expect to be asked.

Solution

The best man team is the perfect answer. You may end up

with more best men than ushers, but it really doesn't matter because there's some overlap of roles anyway. Just be sure they all know exactly what they're doing, especially the one who's in charge of the rings.

Situation
You don't trust the best man either to get your bridegroom to the wedding on time or to make a clean speech at the reception.

Solution
Men usually have strong views about whom they want to be their best man and pressure from the bride on this is one of the chief causes of pre-wedding rows. All you can do is tactfully suggest that your fiancé might like to have more than one best man and hope that his team will include at least one who is more responsible than his first choice. You can also ask for at least one of your own friends or relatives to be an usher and charge them with delivering your husband-to-be to the wedding venue in good condition at the appointed time. Brief your father or another speech maker you know you can trust to be prepared to step in if the best man looks likely to go off the rails and embarrass you. And if you can't trust anyone to step in on your behalf, be prepared to do it yourself!

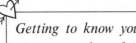

Getting to know your partner's family better will give you a lot of insight into what your partner expects marriage to be like.

THE WEDDING TEAM'S CHECKLIST

☐ However well organised you are, if you and your partner want to feel relaxed enough to enjoy the wedding, you're going to have to depend on your support team. Instead of assuming you'll do everything yourselves and picking key people at random, sit down together and make a list. Write down what you're going to need help with:

- ◆ before the wedding;
- ◆ during the wedding; and
- ◆ after the wedding.

☐ Agree on the key roles, your best man, bridesmaids, your parents and even your ushers and divide the jobs up between them.

☐ Where you have a choice (with the best man and bridesmaids, but obviously not the mothers!) decide who would be best suited to carry out the tasks on the list.

☐ Next, talk to your chosen team, one at a time, to see whether they're up for the responsibilities you've got in mind.

☐ When you have them all lined up, call a team meeting. Inviting them to dinner or lunch is a nice way of doing it but make sure you agree on a firm plan of action before you get too relaxed. Once you've done this, it's a good idea to agree to meet monthly or every six weeks right through to the wedding (it might need to be more often than this as the time draws nearer).

5

Showers, Hen Parties and Stag Nights

Arranging some fun-filled events in the lead-up to your wedding is a good way of motivating your wedding team and of keeping them coming up with good ideas. Pre-wedding celebrations will also mean that, when your wedding day finally arrives, your team will have got to know each other – and that will make for a livelier time for all on the day.

TRADITIONAL PRE-WEDDING CELEBRATIONS

Apart from the reception, the typical British wedding celebrations used to be limited to the engagement party and the bridegroom's stag night. The stag night was always held on the evening before the wedding and had several purposes:

◆ A rite of passage or even an initiation ceremony for young or inexperienced bridegrooms.

◆ A celebration of the last night of being single.

◆ A test of the bridegroom's resolve to get married and his relationship with the bride. It wasn't unknown for bridegrooms to be still drunk at the wedding and, occasionally, not to turn up at all.

Of course, this was a lot more relevant when many bridegrooms were often quite young and still living at home – the stag night could be the first (and last) occasion when a man would be allowed to break all the rules.

Nights in

Hen parties, on the other hand, used to be nights in rather than nights out – evenings when the girls got together to exchange shampoo and nail varnish. There wasn't much point in a final fling when marriage, the height of a woman's ambition, was well and truly within her sights. A wild night out would have been more likely to result in a seriously damaged reputation and even a broken engagement. Sauce for the goose and sauce for the gander were in totally different jars.

PRE-WEDDING CELEBRATIONS TODAY

Now that Britain has become a much more multicultural society, the idea of week-long or at least weekend-long family celebrations has become more popular. Colourful, extended wedding festivities are increasing, replacing traditional stag nights and girls' nights in. This has also got something to do with the fact that more and more people are getting married away from their family home. Brides and grooms are likely to be living independently for years before they get married and they often have more attachment to their own place than their parents' place. And even if the bride does decide to return to her home town, the chances are that the bridegroom may still be coming from somewhere else. For one side of the family at least, as well as a lot of friends, most weddings are long-distance affairs and the guests often decide to make a holiday of it. If they arrive the night before, they might decide to start partying with fellow guests right away – and continue the day after, when the bride and groom are long gone.

But whether customs have changed or whether we're just got more money to spend, there's certainly a lot more to a wedding party than there used to be.

STAG NIGHTS AND HEN PARTIES

A lot of people are deferring the decision to get married until they're older, and they will probably have been leading their own lives and making their own decisions for quite a while before they get married. The trouble with that is that breaking all the rules is a lot more difficult when you've been making and breaking your own rules for ages.

There's not much difference now between a hen party and a stag night, apart from the guest list. So whether you happen to be the bride or the groom, you can use this simple Q&A exercise to help you decide exactly how you want to play it. And playing, of course, is what it's all about, assuming that stag and hen celebrations are really your last chance for a bit of fun before you give up your wild youth to dreary domesticity:

- Is it something I feel I've got to do, or something I really want to do?

- Am I going to choose whom I invite? Is it remotely possible that any of my friends might have sabotage in mind?

- Do I have control over what we do? Or would I rather leave it to chance?

- Is this party my final farewell to a wild and irresponsible lifestyle or is it a taster of the lifestyle I wish I'd had?

When you've answered those questions honestly, to yourself at least, you're ready to start planning.

When are you going to have your stag or hen party and how long is it going to last?

Hardly any bridegrooms and virtually no brides have their party the night before the wedding. Perhaps it's because they're more likely to be getting married out of choice that they prefer to spend the night before looking forward to the future rather than looking back at the past.

The week before the wedding is favourite for one-night parties. But if you're going for a weekend of bonding with your buddies or a week or fortnight's final holiday as a single person, it's probably worth doing it a month or so in advance. Apart from anything else, you may have trouble getting the time off work!

Whom do you invite?

Even some of the most outrageous final fun nights now seem to include same-sex parents and siblings, relatives and even in-laws-to-be as well as friends. This is often the time when you find out who really likes your future partner, who secretly fancies him or her and who dislikes him or her so much that he or she might be considering a last ditch attempt to break up the relationship.

If you plan for your party to be a riotous all-nighter you might consider inviting the older members of the bridal party to the first part only – drinks and dinner perhaps – and send them home for cocoa and an early bed before you hit the hot spots. Or you could have two separate celebrations, an official one to which everyone is invited and an unofficial, off-the-record one for your wilder single friends.

What are the options?

You can do anything you like, but it's considered really tacky to upstage the honeymoon. If you're wealthy enough to think of escaping with your workmates for a week of sun, sea, sand and whatever at a luxury tropical resort, you'd better be sure you take your future spouse to somewhere that's even more glamorous. And it should definitely not be the same place!

Pampering days, weekends and even weeks are popular with brides, and a lot of spas and health farms offer special pre-wedding packages. Apparently, this idea is catching on with some of the blokes as well!

Adrenaline sports and extreme adventures are likely to attract bridegrooms. Parachute jumping, hang gliding and abseiling apparently top the list, with racing-car and go-kart driving, pot holing, diving lessons and mountain climbing also in demand. And, just as the men are catching on to the idea of detox and massage, it appears that a number of brides and bridesmaids are opting for paragliding and survival weekends. Maybe they feel that, if they can get by in the jungle without any make-up or mod cons, organising the wedding is going to be a piece of cake.

Escape and relaxation seem to appeal equally to both sexes. Golfing trips, walking and cycling weekends and sometimes even mini-cruises apparently count as hen and stag parties too. Or you can stick with tradition and go for the drinking, dinner and clubbing option – as posh or as downmarket as you like. But if you're going to be old fashioned about it, don't forget the kit. For brides, this consists of a pair of L-plates, a veil and tiara, and almost anything from Ann Summers. For bridegrooms it's more likely to be purchased from the local joke shop and usually includes a pair of false boobs. The test of a good bachelor bash is apparently not being able to remember it, so if you wake up in the morning – or whenever you wake up – and you can recall enough of it to feel embarrassed, presumably you have to do it all over again. Which is another good reason for leaving plenty of time between stag and hen nights and the wedding itself.

BRIDAL SHOWERS
Bridal showers and rehearsal dinners have been imported from the USA. A shower is a lot like an old-fashioned hen night before the sex and cocktails became compulsory.

It should be a tea party: you invite your girlfriends and they all bring you girly presents, such as garters. It's a gossipy, female-bonding affair where life friendships are reviewed and you can talk about anything you like, including babies. In practice, wine and champagne are often involved, mothers and mother-in-laws are some-times invited and they can turn into long weepy evenings with soppy videos.

BUILDING YOUR SUPPORT GROUP
The most important thing about the single-sex pre-wedding parties is the bonding with your friends. Women seem to be better at asking for emotional confirmation than men, and women seem to have more rituals than the men – like the henna ceremony in Hindu weddings, for example. But bridegrooms probably need this kind of affirmation too. Whether the wedding is a success or a struggle, you may need your friends' support in the future and it's good to know they're going to be there for you.

REHEARSAL DINNERS
The rehearsal never used to be much of a celebration – a quick run through in a cold, empty church followed by an early night for the bride and a riotous stag night for the

groom. But now the rehearsal is often the signal for the start of the festivities and is usually rounded off with lunch or, more usually, dinner for the immediate wedding party.

If you didn't have a formal engagement party, this may be the first meeting of the clans, and rehearsal dinners have provided lots of dramatic and comic moments in films featuring weddings. You can have a private dinner in a restaurant, a meal in the bride's family home or just a takeaway pizza if you want to keep it low key.

PRE-WEDDING BREAKFASTS

These are becoming more and more popular – the bride used to have breakfast in bed, but now she's likely to be sharing it with her mother and bridesmaids while the groom meets his best man and backup team over coffee, eggs and bacon to discuss the day ahead.

TRICKY SITUATIONS

Situation

You want to have a hen party and you'd really like a weekend away at a spa hotel with your best friends. But you can't pay for all of them and some of them simply couldn't afford it.

Solution

Your only solution (apart from limiting the spa weekend to your rich friends only) is to downscale and go for a beauty treatment day, or even an afternoon instead.

Situation

Your colleagues at work want to organise a sailing weekend for your stag party and the boss has offered to lend you his yacht. But your friends from the rugby club want the traditional stag night with a stripper and a visit to a club. You'd prefer the lap-dancing option but your job is important to you and you don't want to offend the boss.

Solution

Be honest with the rugby club – they're your mates, aren't they? Tell them you'll fund a wild stag night on the condition they don't talk about it. Then you can take up the yacht offer as well and your boss will never know. But it does mean you probably can't invite your rugby friends to the wedding because, once they've had a few drinks, they're bound to tell your boss all about the strippergram he missed.

Situation

The rehearsal dinner is getting out of hand. Besides yourself and the bride, there are both sets of parents, the vicar, the witnesses, the best man team and the ushers and the bridesmaids and all their prospective partners. You had booked a private table at a very nice restaurant but, with numbers at 25 and rising and nobody else offering to share the costs, you are thinking of relocating to the kebab shop.

Solution

This is the kind of situation that can arise at any stage in the wedding celebrations. For a rehearsal dinner, you can ask for contributions from both sets of parents but you can't really expect anyone else to pay because in theory they are all doing you a favour by helping out with your wedding. If you can't afford it, you can either cancel or cut back. If it's summer and the weather's good, how about a champagne picnic with takeaway food? If it's winter you could do the same at somebody's house. If you can't find anywhere to share a takeaway, invite everybody for a bar meal at the local pub instead.

Situation

Your girlfriends are planning your hen night party and some of them are likely to have some pretty wild ideas. You're sure it's going to be embarrassing and you don't really want to do anything you'll regret.

Solution

There's no reason why you have to stay to the bitter end of a hen night if you really don't want to. Organise transport for yourself (one girl had her step-mother standing by to drive her home) or have enough money for a taxi and the number of a good cab firm in the area. If the party takes a turn for the worse and you aren't having fun, pretend to be very sick and head home. They can tell you all about it in the morning so you'll get the highlights without the headache.

Don't waste your energy trying to change the person you married. If there's something you don't like, all you can change is your response to it.

PRE-WEDDING CELEBRATIONS CHECKLIST

☐ Organising some fun events in the lead-up to the wedding is a good way to keep your team motivated and buzzing with good ideas. It also means that, when the wedding comes along, the core crew will have got to know each other and that always makes for a livelier party on the day.

☐ Before you organise or agree to any pre-wedding event, ask yourself if you expect to enjoy it more than you'll regret it.

$$\textcircled{6}$$

The Wedding

Your wedding day is the day your support team will be put to the ultimate test. It is also the day to start delegating, if you haven't already done so. But before you hand everything over to your wedding team, give yourself plenty of time to sit down and call every supplier you'll be using on the day just to reassure yourself everything is ready and in order.

TRADITIONAL WEDDING PATTERNS

When a church wedding was the only option, the ceremony was very straightforward. Every wedding, rich or poor, was always basically the same:

◆ The wedding rehearsal would have taken place one or two days ahead of time so that the priest could explain the order of service to the bride and groom, the best man and the couple's parents, and perhaps even the bridesmaids and ushers as well.

◆ First to arrive on the day would be the ushers, ready to greet and direct the early guests. The bride's family would always take the left-hand side of the church with the groom's family on the right. Close family sat in the front row(s) with other relatives immediately behind them and friends filling up the space at the back on both sides.

◆ The best man and bridegroom would be in their places at least 20 minutes ahead of time. They would wait at the chancel steps, on the right-hand side of the church, in front of the groom's family and guests. The best man would stand to the right and slightly behind the bridegroom, who could then turn to the bride on his left.

◆ Close family, especially the groom's parents, would also be early.

◆ Ten minutes or so before the start of the ceremony the bridesmaids would arrive with the bride's mother. The mother would take her place at the front of the other guests while the bridesmaids waited outside for the bride with at least one of the ushers.

- If it was a big, formal wedding, the priest would probably wait with the bridesmaids at the church door.

- At the right time, or a little later, the bride would arrive with her father. After a moment or two for the bridesmaids to help her with her hair or her veil (her face would be covered at this stage), she would take her father's right arm, ready to walk up the aisle. The priest and choir would walk ahead of her and her bridesmaids; flower girls and pages would follow.

- At this point, the usher would go to the organist and tell him to play the entrance music. This was the signal for the congregation to stand.

- When she arrived at the chancel steps with her father, the bride would lift her veil and stand to the left of the bridegroom with her father on her left and slightly behind her.

- From that point, the priest would direct the service. After the bride's father had been called upon to give her away he would step back and sit down with his wife in the front pew. After handing over the rings, the best man would also step back and sit in the bridegroom's family front pew.

- Following the service and signing the register, the bride would walk back down the aisle on the left arm of the bridegroom, followed by her father escorting the bridegroom's mother, the bridegroom's father escorting the bride's mother and the chief bridesmaid on the arm of the best man.

WEDDING PATTERNS TODAY

Even if you are having a Church of England wedding, you might not necessarily want to follow this format quite so precisely. But whatever kind of ceremony you decide to have, you might like to take something from the rituals of the old wedding service.

MAKING IT SPECIAL

In the flurry of wedding clothes, wedding presents and table arrangements, it's easy to forget what a major commitment you've taken on. A generation or two ago, people didn't have much choice about getting married – it was really the only option for raising children in the social mainstream. Living independently, especially with children, was only an option if you were either extremely rich and eccentric, or utterly destitute.

But, for most people today, the decision to get married is a completely free choice – and, in fact, it's becoming an increasingly unusual choice as well. Being a single parent is acceptable and so is living alone. So if you decide to get married, you've probably got some very strong personal reasons and convictions about it and that makes the ceremony more significant than ever before.

It's easy to neglect the symbolism and rituals of marriage but, even if you're having the simplest of register office weddings, you might want to think about how you can make it more memorable and meaningful.

WORDS

Whether you're having a church wedding, a civil wedding or any other kind of religious ceremony, you will find there is usually a basic core of vows or declarations which have to be made verbally before the register is signed.

If it's a Church of England wedding, you can choose one of three versions of the service you like best. The bride doesn't have to promise to obey her husband any more but, if she does, the bridegroom must promise to cherish her in return.

A register office wedding is the shortest and simplest ceremony you can have. It takes 15 minutes or less and there's not usually any leeway for individual touches. You could always personalise the occasion afterwards, perhaps at the beginning of the reception, by setting up some rituals of your own and perhaps exchanging some vows you have composed for each other.

A wedding at a licensed venue is often more flexible in terms of format, but you will still be limited by the amount of time the registrar is able to attend. Find out how much time you will have in the actual wedding room after the registrar has left and then, while you still have all your guests sitting down together, you may be able to add your own words and music.

Besides the usual Bible passages about love, there are plenty of other favourite wedding poems and readings (see Chapter 10). But you might want to choose some more unusual ones that are special to you, or even write something for yourself.

MUSIC

Music has always been associated with weddings and you can make even the simplest ceremony more beautiful if you set it to music.

Wedding bells

Wedding bells are a symbol of good luck. If you are getting married in church, ask the priest in advance if you want the bell ringers to turn out for you (they will probably need paying). If it's a civil ceremony you could get some hand-bell ringers to give you a few peals afterwards while your family and friends are throwing confetti.

Choirs and organists

A choir and organist are usually available for a church wedding but, like the bell ringers, they are probably an optional extra. If you're planning to have hymns you will certainly need the organist and, if your guests aren't regular churchgoers, the choir can turn the singing from an embarrassment into a beautiful experience. They will also sing during any gaps in the service, such as the signing of the register and waiting for the bride to arrive.

Soloists

Soloists (either singers or instrumentalists) are another option, especially if you aren't getting married in church – although you can usually take your own musicians to church as well. There are plenty of them who specialise in both wedding ceremonies and wedding receptions. Harpists and string quartets are popular, probably because they're relaxing to listen to but, if you're wanting something livelier, you might consider a fiddler or guitar players.

WEDDING SYMBOLS

Exchanging rings

Exchanging rings is a part of most wedding rituals. Rings have no beginning and no end – they are a symbol of completeness and eternal commitment. In some traditions, other pieces of jewellery are sometimes exchanged – even handwritten promises locked away in small boxes or lockets. Tattoos and vials of each other's blood have had a lot of publicity lately, but they are probably best exchanged privately.

Candles

Candles have always been involved in all kinds of rituals, the flame being a symbol of life, love and passion. Some churches use three wedding candles: a large candle symbolising the marriage is lit by the person in charge of the ceremony and two smaller candles, one for the bride and one for the groom, which are then lit from the larger candle.

Flowers

Bride's flowers
The bride's flowers symbolise innocence and purity although they are more likely to be chosen because they go well with the dress.

Flowers for the wedding party
Flowers for the wedding party are usually provided by the bride's family, with buttonholes for the men and corsages for the ladies. The buttonholes for the bridegroom, best man, ushers and fathers of the bridal couple will usually match the bride's bouquet, or at least the general wedding

colour scheme. For the bride and bridegroom's mothers and grandmothers it's best to provide white flowers or flowers which tone in with their outfits. And, if your budget will stretch that far, it's a nice touch to give one of the ushers a basket of buttonholes for all the guests – especially if it's a summer wedding.

Flowers for the ceremony and reception
Flowers for both the wedding ceremony and the reception can be expensive, so see if you can share the cost of decorating the church or wedding room with another wedding couple. Alternatively, you might be able to take some of the arrangements with you from the ceremony to the reception. If it's a church wedding there are usually some flower arrangers at the church who may be willing to help you. They will have all the vases and equipment as well as the expertise and perhaps even some tips about where to buy the flowers more cheaply.

The meanings of flowers
The meanings of flowers are lovely and there are bound to be some that will fit your personal colour scheme:

Bluebells – lasting love
Carnations – woman in love
Chrysanthemums (red) – I love you
Chrysanthemums (white) – truth
Daffodils – regard
Daises – innocence
Ferns – sincerity
Forget-me-nots – true love
Geraniums – true friendship
Holly – enchantment

Honeysuckle – bonds of love
Ivy – fidelity
Jasmine – sensuality
Lemon blossom – fidelity
Lilac – first emotions
Lily-of-the-valley – happiness
Lilies – ardour
Myrtle – love
Rose – romance
Snowdrops – hope
Sweet peas – lasting pleasures
Tulips – declaration of love

Confetti

Confetti symbolises the flower-strewn path of happily married life. It's fun, it's pretty and it makes a great photograph, but check whether or not it's allowed at your venue. You can now buy biodegradable confetti or, better still, real flower petals, which won't cause a litter problem wherever you throw them.

Transport

Transport for the bride and groom is also important because it symbolises the journey from one way of life to another as well as the journey of marriage which the couple are about to make. This is why people beg, borrow or pay a fortune for romantic, glamorous or exotic cars and carriages for their special day.

The bride and her father, and sometimes the bridesmaids as well, usually arrive in the special vehicle which then waits to take the bride and groom to the reception. Think about the practicality of it before you make your final decision – open carriages look wonderful, but you need to be pretty sure about the weather. Stretch limousines are popular at the moment but are probably a better choice for the hen night than the wedding because the windows are blacked out. There's no point in driving to your wedding in style if nobody can see you!

PRACTICAL MATTERS: BEFORE THE WEDDING

The venue
Check the venue is big enough for all your guests to be comfortably seated and that any elderly people can be accommodated. Also see whether it will be easy for people with small children to slip out without disturbing every-one else.

Invitations
Invitations do a lot more than just tell people about the time and date:

◆ The design of the invitations gives the guests a sense of the style of the wedding and perhaps even an idea of what to wear.

◆ They should include not only a map and directions to both the wedding and the reception but also informa-tion about flights and ferries if the wedding is abroad.

◆ There should also be a list of B&Bs and hotels ranging from budget to expensive and perhaps even a guide to the area for guests who are coming from a long distance away.

- A note asking if anyone is on a special diet or needs extra facilities is also a very thoughtful touch.

- Give clear instructions about whether small children are invited and if there will be a crèche or babysitting facilities and children's meals.

- It's up to you whether you include the wedding list or just a note saying that it's available on request.

- Make it very clear that you expect a reply in good time, regardless of whether the invitation is accepted or not. It used to be considered rude to include a reply card but this is now quite a usual thing to do.

- If you are juggling the numbers, send out a personal pre-wedding notice with the date and venue and ask people to give you an idea of whether or not they'd be able to come. This will help you draw up your final list without agonising over the people who wouldn't be able to make it anyway. It will also give you advance warning about the people you hoped would refuse but who seem determined to turn up regardless.

- If you are inviting some people simply for drinks and dancing or perhaps a buffet after the main celebration, you will need completely separate invitations. Make it clear whether or not they are to expect food and make sure that the wedding meal is cleared away before they arrive so that you can greet them properly and they won't feel as though they have missed out on something.

Rehearsals

Rehearsals aren't just an excuse for a dinner party. It's a good idea to rehearse even if you aren't having a church wedding. Get together with your wedding party just before the day and walk through exactly who is doing what and how long it takes. The bride and groom and probably some of the other people involved are likely to be nervous and it helps a lot if you've all been through it in advance. Borrowing the actual room you'll be using, just for half an hour or so, is much the best option but, if you can't do that, make sure you have a run-through on the order of the ceremony and sort out who stands where and who says what.

PRACTICAL MATTERS: DURING THE WEDDING

The register

Signing the register sounds simple enough and whoever officiates at your wedding will talk you through this at the time. But remember that you'll be signing your full name, with all your first names, which is probably not the signature you'd normally use. You might like to try it out a couple of times beforehand if you think you're likely to wobble on it.

You will need two witnesses who must be over the age of 18 and legally sane. The witnesses don't have to sign their full name and can use their usual signature.

The very young and the elderly

Very young and very elderly relatives need to be comfortable. Get the ushers to seat the older ones where they have plenty of space and can get comfortable and provide some picture books and quiet toys for the tiny tots.

PRACTICAL MATTERS: AFTER THE WEDDING

Photographs

Photographs are an important (and potentially very expensive) part of the wedding. They are often taken for granted but, unless your photographer is carefully chosen and well briefed, the photography can seriously disrupt the proceedings. Standing outside a church on a cold windy afternoon for half an hour or more while the photographer lines up group after group of shivering guests can be a miserable experience. There are various steps you can take to avoid this happening.

Reportage

Reportage photography is becoming more and more popular. The photographer, often starting well before the wedding, takes informal shots of groups and individuals. The bride and group can still have the basic group portraits if they want them, but there will be more photos of informal clusters of people at all stages of the wedding party.

Reportage tends to be more expensive because many more shots are taken and the photographer is present for much longer and generally requires more skill and experience.

Indoor groups

Indoor group photographs are another alternative if the weather isn't good. It's best to line people up either while they are still in the church or the wedding room or at the very beginning of the reception before they start looking dishevelled. If you want to do this, check that the photographer will bring the necessary lighting and equipment for indoor photography.

Providing entertainment

Entertaining the guests who are not actually being photographed is another option. This is a good reason for taking most of the formal photographs at the reception venue and perhaps providing some live music so that guests can be given a drink in comfortable surroundings without getting cold and bored.

After the wedding

After the wedding a lot of the guests might like to see the official photographs and some will want to order a copy of one or two of them. Talk to the photographer about this – he or she may supply an album of proofs that can be passed or posted around and may also be able to make them available on the Internet. This is obviously the easiest option for a lot of people who may even be able to order online as well, directly from the photographer.

Moving from the wedding to the reception

Getting to the reception can sometimes be a problem and, if there's going to be any kind of gap between your wedding and your reception, in terms of either time or distance, put some thought into making sure everything runs smoothly. Everyone should have a map or directions with his or her invitation, but have some spare ones to hand in case somebody has lost one or left it behind. It's important that nobody is left hanging around or feeling uncertain. Unless you specifically state on the invitation that guests will be left to their own devices for a couple of hours at some stage, it's your responsibility to look after them throughout the day. One of the ushers should go to the reception venue immediately after the wedding to look after any guests who get fed up with the photos and arrive before you.

TRICKY SITUATIONS

Situation
Your father is gay and is now living with his boyfriend. He wants his boyfriend to be involved in the wedding but, although you are fond of them both, you can't see a way of doing this.

Solution
You could perhaps ask whether it's possible for them both to give you away (assuming you want to be given away, of course). You take your father's right arm and his boyfriend's left arm. Otherwise you could ask the boyfriend to be an usher or a witness, do a reading at the ceremony or make a speech at the reception. Before you make any decision at all, think about whether this would offend anybody else who matters to you. During the course of a wedding somebody, somewhere is always bound to be offended – you can't please everybody and it's your day – but if your mother (for example) would be distressed by your father's boyfriend having a high-profile role, you might want to take this into consideration.

Situation
One of you is a Catholic, the other is a member of the Church of England and both sides of the family want the wedding to be in their own church.

Solution
In theory it's the bride who chooses where she wants to be married. But when a couple are coming from very different religious backgrounds it generally depends on who has the stronger conviction and whether or not you

intend to stay with your religion and raise your children in it after marriage.

Similar problems arise with all cross-faith marriages and, as these are happening more and more often, some religious organisations are becoming more co-operative and flexible about mixed wedding arrangements. Find out what your particular churches will allow and make sure you really understand the importance of your partner's background to him or her:

◆ Some religions (Catholic and Church of England, for example) will conduct joint ceremonies although usually only one of the priests will actually perform the key part of the wedding. Go directly to your priest or minister to find out about this.

◆ Perhaps the answer could be two separate ceremonies, preferably close together so that you can have just one reception afterwards.

◆ If you are not particularly religious, a civil ceremony followed by a blessing (or two) might be the answer.

◆ If the two families are so far apart on religious grounds that they would not attend the other's church or temple, you might consider having the blessings on different days, followed by a smaller celebration for the two different families.

Situation
Both you and your fiancé(e)'s parents have remarried so there are four parent couples instead of two. Do they all sit in the front row?

Solution

It depends on three things:

- how big the front row is;

- how well they get on with their exes; and

- most important of all, how you and your fiancé(e) feel about it.

The correct solution is for the natural parents to sit together in the front row with their current spouses sitting directly behind them. But weddings are emotional events and often stir up long-forgotten feelings, both positive and negative. There's no point in sticking to the rules if they are going to upset more people than breaking them would do. The chances are that somebody, somewhere is going to feel bad, but you may have to ask your family to be on their best behaviour, just for the day.

Men and women are from different planets. You and your partner will handle emotional situations differently. For example, when women are unhappy, they may need sympathy rather than immediate action. When men get anxious they like to talk through potential solutions.

WEDDING CHECKLIST

☐ This is the time to put your support team to the test and, if you haven't done so already, start delegating. But before you hand it all over, take the time to sit down and call every supplier you'll be using on the day, just to reassure yourself that they're all lined up and ready to go.

☐ During the week leading up to the wedding, make sure you have at least one evening with your partner, just the two of you, where you can quietly talk through the wedding arrangements and think about the future.

☐ Make sure you've both tried on your wedding outfits. If you're the bride, remember to leave out one item for luck.

☐ Allow some pampering time just before the wedding to make sure you're rested and looking your best.

☐ And last, but not least, have some breakfast before the wedding breakfast. Champagne on an empty stomach is going to slow you down and this will be the longest (and shortest) day of your life.

7

The Reception

Before you arrange anything, find out if you both have the same priorities for what makes a successful wedding reception: the food, venue, drinks or the entertainment? If you each have different ideas about what makes for a successful reception, agree on a compromise before you choose the venue or make any other big and expensive decisions.

TRADITIONAL RECEPTIONS

It used to be called a wedding breakfast because, however late in the day it was held, it was assumed that the bride would be too sick with nerves and that the bridegroom would be too sick from the stag night for either of them to have eaten beforehand.

After the wedding, usually held in a church, everybody would go to a different location for the reception. The bride and bridegroom and their families formed a 'receiving line' to greet their guests and there was a strict order for this:

◆ bride's mother
◆ groom's father
◆ groom's mother
◆ bride's father
◆ bride
◆ groom
◆ chief bridesmaid
◆ best man.

Next, the guests would be offered a drink, usually sherry, before being shown the seating plan and invited to go to their tables. The procession into the dining room was the same as the procession after the wedding ceremony:

◆ bride and groom
◆ bride's father with groom's mother
◆ bride's mother with groom's father
◆ chief bridesmaid with best man.

The seating plan, like the receiving line, was always the same. The top table faced the other tables and, from the right, the seating arrangement would be:

◆ groom's mother
◆ bride's father
◆ bride
◆ bridegroom
◆ bride's mother
◆ groom's father
◆ chief bridesmaid
◆ best man.

At the other tables, all facing the top table, the bride's family would be seated on the right and the groom's family on the left with friends towards the back. If the priest who conducted the wedding was present he would be asked to say grace before the meal. At the end, the best man, or toastmaster, would introduce the speeches in this order:

◆ The bride's father, with a toast to the bride and groom.

◆ The bridegroom, who would thank the bride's parents and all the guests for coming, toast the bridesmaids and present them with their gifts.

◆ The best man, who would thank the groom on behalf of the bridesmaids and read out the cards and messages.

The cutting of the cake followed the speeches. The bride held the knife in her right hand, with the bridegroom's right hand on hers. The cake was then taken into the kitchen. Some was cut into slices for the guests to eat with their coffee and some was packed into boxes to send to the guests who couldn't come to the wedding. The top tier was saved for the christening.

If there was to be dancing, the bride and groom would lead the first dance with the best man and chief bridesmaid joining in half-way through. Finally, the bride and groom used always to leave before their guests, having first changed into their going-away outfits. Just before leaving, the bride would turn her back on the group and throw her bouquet over her shoulder. The single female who caught it would be the next bride.

RECEPTIONS TODAY

Things have changed a lot. Receptions can be as wildly different as you like, with the emphasis often on the wild. But even the most exotic of wedding receptions usually includes at least one or two of the more sedate traditions of the past.

One big difference, of course, is that now many hotels and other buildings are licensed for weddings and so the ceremony is often in the same location as the reception. This cuts out a lot of the problems that used to be caused by having too much of a break between the wedding itself and the party afterwards. It wasn't unusual to have a space of several miles or several hours between the two parts of the wedding, and guests often lost either themselves or their party spirit in the gap.

CHOOSING THE VENUE

The first thing to decide is where you'd like to be married and whether you want to have the reception in the same place. A Church of England or register office wedding rules out this possibility unless you book the church hall or the town hall.

The key criteria for choosing a venue are usually budget and ambience.

Budget

The reception is one of the obvious places to cut costs if your budget looks like getting out of hand.

Self-catering

A self-catering buffet is the cheapest option, but it means hiring a venue with a kitchen you can use and plenty of fridge space so that you can prepare food the day before. You also need to be sure that you can get all the help you need both beforehand and on the day. Even with a buffet, you'll need help with serving food and drinks unless your family and guests are happy to run around with trays on the day. This means hiring waiters and bar staff.

Drinks

Saving money on drinks is possible if you hire a hall and self-cater. On the other hand, if you do that, you don't have the option of a paying bar to fall back on later in the evening.

Menu options

Check all the menu options because even the grandest venues have a range of prices per head. And if you've invited more guests after the main meal, you need to find out how much you'll be charged for a late-night buffet.

Time of year

Take the time of year into account. Getting married in summer is more expensive. You may find you can afford a more glamorous reception if you don't mind taking a chance on the weather and going for a date in November or February. It's also easier in winter to make a very average venue look glamorous with lots of fairy lights and candles. Darkness hides a multitude of dull furnishing and depressing paintwork.

Ambience

The following are some things you might like to consider about the venue's ambience:

◆ *What suits your wedding style?* An old building with atmosphere or a new one with dramatic spaces?

◆ *How important is the outdoor area?* If it's a summer wedding, are you looking for a picturesque garden or gazebo for drinks and photographs?

◆ *What about something completely different?* A marquee, a special themed venue like an amusement park or a zoo, botanical gardens or stately home?

◆ *What time of day and time of year is your wedding?* Do you need somewhere that will look good on a bad day? Or by candlelight? Is the interior more important than the exterior?

◆ *How flexible do you need the venue to be?*
  – A large or small dance floor?
  – Space for people to have drinks and mingle before going in to the wedding meal?

- A quiet sitting-out area for the older people? They may well want to sit down for a while as soon as they get to the reception, especially if they have been standing up for the photos.

- A children's room with play space and TV? If there are likely to be a lot of people with small children it may be worth hiring an entertainer and feeding the children separately so that they don't get bored and disruptive.

- Are the bathrooms adequate?

- Is there a staffed cloakroom?

- Somewhere to display the wedding presents?

You could sit down with your partner and prepare your own checklist – with perhaps some help from mothers or other financially interested parties. This makes the final decision much simpler because you can count up the ticks and go for the one that has the most.

SETTING UP THE VENUE

Some venues will allow you a completely free hand while others will be restrictive about where you can put flowers and what sort of lighting you can have. If you choose a romantic mediaeval castle, a few lilies and candles will probably be all it needs. But if your budget limits you to the local village hall, you'll might need to be more creative.

Flowers

You can't have too many flowers at a wedding, but they can be incredibly expensive. The bride's bouquet alone might cost between £50 and £100, so think carefully about what you want and whom you want to arrange them.

◆ See if you can bring some arrangements with you from the ceremony to the reception so that you get more value from them. You might even be able to hire green plants from the local nursery – it's worth a try.

◆ Use seasonal flowers – ask the florist what would be the best value for the time of year.

◆ Sometimes the colour is more important than the actual flowers in arrangements that will only be seen from a distance. You might be able to substitute cheaper ones (usually carnations and chrysanthemums) for more expensive ones.

◆ You can make a few flowers go a long way with lots of ribbon and greenery.

◆ If it's winter, especially around Christmas and New Year, think about using painted twigs and berries as well as plenty of holly and ivy.

◆ If you have access to large amounts of evergreen foliage, it can be an amazingly effective cover-up for a less than perfect venue – My son was lucky enough to be loaned a beautiful house in the Caribbean for his wedding but the owner failed to mention that major building works were being carried out at the time. It took three days of hard work by all the guests to scrub and rebuild and to connect up the electricity and gas and, one day before the wedding, there were still gaping holes in the masonry. Camouflage was the answer and a team of palm weavers moved in to create huge green panels which covered all the remaining gaps. It's amazing what you can do with a bit of greenery.

Candles and fairy lights

Next to flowers, it's lighting that turns an ordinary room into a romantic setting. If your reception will be held after dark, make an advance visit to see how the rooms are normally lit for a party. Then you can decide what you need to do to create the atmosphere you want. Talk to the premises manager about the effect you're hoping to achieve and see what's possible. If they specialise in wedding parties they will probably be able to help you decorate the room and set the tables to match your chosen theme.

Table decorations

There is an almost infinite amount of stuff you can put on the table, from sparkling confetti, traditional bags of almonds for the guests, napkin bows, feathers and elaborate place cards to individual flower arrangements and tea lights. If you look at some of the pictures in the wedding magazines you will notice that there isn't much room for plates and knives and forks. If you enjoy that kind of detail you can have some fun with it. If you don't, simplicity could be your personal style statement.

ON THE DAY

The receiving line

This may sound like an old-fashioned idea but it's a good way to make sure every single guest is welcomed and that his or her needs are taken care of. You may not want to be rigid about who stands where in the receiving line, but obviously the bride and groom should be at the front. It's also a good idea to mix the two families and the generations as well so that everyone has a good chance of being recognised as he or she is being greeted. It's best to have the receiving line at the entrance to the reception so that you catch everybody, but if the bride and groom are delayed for any reason you can always do the meeting and greeting at the entrance to the dining room, between the initial drinks and dinner.

Drinks

This is a very controversial subject at weddings unless, of course, you're teetotal, which makes it easy (and cheap). Whatever you do, it's very important to offer guests a drink as soon as they arrive at the reception. In fact, if you have some of the posed photographs taken at the reception it's much easier on your guests because they will be more relaxed – and refreshed – while they're waiting to line up and smile.

Water and soft drinks
These should be freely available throughout the reception.

Greetings drinks
Greeting drinks should be accompanied by canapés or something to nibble, especially if there's likely to be much of a gap before the meal is served. A lot of potentially nervous and emotional people drinking on empty stomachs is a recipe for disaster. Some guests will have travelled long distances and the wedding party may not have felt like eating much breakfast.

Greeting drinks should also include something hot if it's winter. The older members of the party may be much more delighted with a cup of tea than with champagne.

Champagne or sparkling wine
Champagne or sparkling wine is usually offered as a first drink as well as being brought out again for the toasts and the cutting of the cake. If you're having it at the beginning, include a choice of orange juice, buck's fizz and water. And perhaps sherry as well for the older guests.

Of course, it's glamorous to serve champagne throughout the entire reception but, if you do, there should also be red and white wine with the meal. If you're on a budget but you want to stay fizzy, good-quality sparkling wine is much cheaper than champagne. Most people won't notice after they've had a couple.

Wine
Wine is a cheaper option than champagne, especially if you can source some good, basic plonk. Of course, it may take some research to find exactly what you want at a reasonable price, but you'll probably be able to get your wedding team to help. If you decide to serve it from the start of the reception you need only introduce sparkling stuff for the toasts and the cake.

Cocktails and mixed drinks
These might be fun if your reception has a theme to it. If it's a summer garden party you could serve jugs of Pimms or, if you hire a steel band and go for a Caribbean atmosphere, you could have rum punch.

Spirits

Spirits aren't usually provided for free, unless money is truly no object in which case you may as well go the whole hog and have a vodka luge. The weddings most likely to get out of hand are the ones where people are drinking unaccustomed doubles all night – which is OK of course, if it's what you want.

Paying bars

Paying bars may seem like the only option if you're broke, but it's not one I'd recommend. These people are your guests and, if you can't even offer them a drink, perhaps it's worth considering how you might cut costs somewhere else. The first few drinks should be free, even if you run a paying bar for spirits and cocktails.

After-dinner guests

After dinner guests should also be offered a glass of wine or champagne. After all, they missed out on the main reception and if you care enough about them to invite them, they should be given the chance to toast your future at your expense.

The wedding meal

There are absolutely no rules about wedding meals any more, and you can do anything you like from ordering fish-and-chip suppers in newspaper to an eight-course dinner in a private room at the most expensive restaurant in town:

♦ Decide what you want to spend per head and work from there.

- Unless it's a very small party and you know everybody very well, it's a good idea to provide a vegetarian option and check whether anyone has allergies or special dietary requirements.

- If children are invited, make sure there's a children's menu.

- It's better to have a simple meal exquisitely prepared than an elaborate one badly cooked. If you're hiring a caterer, be guided by the menus they show you. There's no point in asking them to provide something that's clearly way beyond their normal capability because they are likely to let you down.

- Most hotels will let you try out your wedding menu. Book in advance for a small party – your wedding team, perhaps, or your parents – and ask the chef to prepare your wedding meal.

The seating plan

The only way to avoid having to work out a seating plan is to have a buffet and let people sit where they want. Even if it's a buffet, the bride and groom and the rest of the wedding party don't usually have to queue up with everybody else for their plate of smoked salmon or salad – they can expect to be served. It does mean, though, that they can move around among the other tables, perhaps eating each course with a different group.

On the other hand, a seating plan has its advantages:

♦ It makes life a lot easier for the people who don't really know anyone else and are shy about where to sit.

♦ You can mix the families together (as long as you think they will cope with this), which helps people get to know each other and generally makes the party more fun.

♦ And you can also keep any troublemakers well apart.

Speeches
Larger, formal weddings sometimes still hire a toastmaster or master of ceremonies and there are plenty of them on the wedding circuit (see Chapter 12). The toastmaster makes all the announcements right from the first round of drinks, directing guests to dinner and introducing the speakers and entertainers. It makes life easy because you know that everything will happen on time and just as you intended, and it relieves the best man of a lot of responsibility. On the downside, it can seem rather impersonal. (For more about speeches, see Chapter 9.)

The cake
A wedding cake used to mean a three-tiered fruitcake covered in almond paste and hard royal icing, formally decorated with piped edges and a model of a bride and groom on the top. But now, that's just about the only kind of cake that *isn't* currently fashionable. A wedding cake can be anything from a pile of fairy cakes to a castle made out of chocolate.

A multi-purpose cake, such as a cheesecake or croquen-bouche, will save you money because you can substitute it for the pudding at the wedding meal. The drawback is that you can't save any for a christening and you can't post it out to all your elderly relatives. If you do want a traditional cake, you might be able to cut costs by getting your mother or your auntie to make it and then get it professionally iced – call the British Sugarcraft Guild if you want to find out more about that idea (see Chapter 12).

The cake cutting is a great photo opportunity and, in America, the bride feeds a piece of cake to the groom as a sign that she accepts her duty to provide him with three square meals a day for the rest of his life.

The late buffet

If you're having a two-part wedding with some people invited to the main meal and others to drinks and dancing afterwards, it's a good idea to provide a light buffet later on. Sandwiches and, of course, wedding cake are not expensive – although you can put on something much fancier if you want to.

Coffee

It's a nice idea to provide coffee and, perhaps, some other hot drinks, late in the evening. The people who have to drive home and the ones who want to stay awake and party for longer will really appreciate it.

Photographs

Now that the photos aren't just confined to groups outside the church, you might find you also have an 'alternative' album of after-the-wedding shots. This is especially so if you go for the currently fashionable practice of putting disposable cameras on the tables and asking the guests to hand them in when they've used up the film.

Music, dancing and entertainment

You can use music to create any atmosphere you want, to inspire you during the ceremony, to relax everyone afterwards and to get them dancing when they've had dinner. Like flowers, this can be expensive, so spend some time first thinking through the various options.

Music at the ceremony

This is a nice optional extra which makes everyone feel good, encourages them to sing and fills the gaps. If it's a church wedding you'll probably be able to get the choir, organist and bell ringers for a modest fee.

Music with the drinks

Music with the drinks at the start of the reception is a lovely way of setting the scene for the party but it's not absolutely essential. People usually find it easy to talk to each other at that stage because they aren't too tired, they've just got their first drink and they are eager to either discuss what you were wearing or catch up on the football results they missed while the wedding was taking place.

Music during the meal

This is less important, because you want it to be quiet enough for people to be able to talk easily to each other without having to shout.

Music after the meal

This is the most important music to provide, especially if you want the party to last. You might consider having a band for three or four hours, followed by a disco if you want the party to go on into the night. If you're on a tight budget you could hire a disco with a DJ for the whole evening.

Choosing your band or DJ
This takes time and research. Always see them in action before you book them and check whether they can vary their style according to the venue.

Most multipurpose bands who specialise in this kind of function can play in a wide range of styles and can turn out as a ten piece or a three piece according to what you pay for. This kind of flexibility also means that, if one of them is unwell on the day, they can probably bring on a substitute. Make sure the DJ has a good selection of the kind of music you want.

Audience participation
Audience participation often gets the party going. Find out in advance if there's anybody who would be willing to sing or play an instrument and see if he or she would like to do a few solos. And if you're having a DJ, ask everyone to list their three favourite songs when they reply to the wedding invitation – that way you're sure of having music everybody likes.

Dancing
Dancing in a more formal way is getting to be popular again, so you might consider hiring a dancing teacher as well the band and having a salsa or ballroom-dancing session for your wedding. You could mention it on the invitations so that your guest can take a few lessons if they like the idea. It's surprising how quickly you can get people up and dancing.

Giving the bride and groom a good send-off
The bride and groom don't always leave before the end of the reception as they used to do. As one bride said, 'how often do I get all my family and friends in one place,

having a good time – and all because of me! Why on earth would I want to miss out on the fun?'

This means there's less of an opportunity for a grand farewell with all the guests waving the couple off in their balloon-covered car for the trip of a lifetime. And it also means that the bride sometimes forgets about her bouquet so, if you're the bride and you're staying until the end of your party, remember to throw your flowers. The best time to do it is just before people sit down to eat.

TRICKY SITUATIONS

Situation
Is it rude to have a reserve list for the reception?

Solution
It's very upsetting when someone you only invited out of duty drops out, leaving you with an empty place you could have filled with someone you like. The answer is to do your invitations in two stages. First, send a note to all the people you feel you *ought* to invite. At this stage, although it isn't an invitation, you make it clear that if they can't make a firm commitment you won't be sending an invitation. (There are nice ways of doing this – see Chapter 9.)

Situation
Should you invite relatives ahead of friends if numbers at the reception are limited?

Solution
Are these relatives you really care about? Or relatives you feel a duty towards? Will you ever see them again? How

long term are the friendships? Difficult, isn't it! The classic solution is to invite the relatives to the formal meal and speeches and then send out a separate invitation to your friends for the dancing, drinks and buffet supper later.

Situation
If your parents haven't spoken to each other since you were in junior school, do they still have to sit next to each other at the reception?

Solution
There are all sorts of variations on this particular theme. It could be just as easily your parents' new spouses who don't get on or even some more distant relatives. In a situation like this, it's probably best not to have a top table. Either make a seating plan which ensures that people only sit next to people they like, or forget the seating plan and let them sort it out for themselves.

Situation
If your parents have been married several times can you invite all their exes if you get on well with them?

Solution
It depends how well they get on with each other. If it isn't emotionally sensitive, go right ahead. If, on the other hand, it's likely to cause trouble, you might want to stick with inviting just the current partners. If you do that, you can acknowledge the special relationship you have with your ex-stepmothers or ex-stepfathers by paying them a visit before the wedding and perhaps having dinner with them separately.

Marriage is an adventure, not a safety net.

RECEPTION CHECKLIST

☐ Think back over all the weddings you've ever been to. What were the best bits? Where did you get bored? What worked and what didn't?

☐ What sort of time do you want your guests to have at your wedding? Happy and relaxed? Wildly exciting? Elegant and sophisticated? Glamorous and glitzy?

☐ How are you going to make sure that each and every one of your guests has a good time?

☐ Will you be inviting anybody who might give somebody else a hard time? How are you going to defuse this situation in advance? By not inviting one of them? Or doing some pre-wedding diplomacy?

☐ What are your priorities:
  ◆ The food?
  ◆ The venue?
  ◆ The drinks?
  ◆ The entertainment?

When the two of you have gone through this list, ask yourselves if you both have the same priorities. If it turns out that you each have rather different ideas about what makes a successful wedding reception, it's a good idea to agree on a compromise before you choose the venue or make any other big and expensive decisions.

8

Making your Wedding Legal

Marriage is a public emotional commitment and you can be married to anyone, by anyone, at any time and in any place you like. But if you want the marriage to be recognised by the UK and other governments it must be performed by someone who is licensed by the state to enter it in the national Register of Births, Deaths and Marriages.

The same basic rules and conditions apply to all marriages, whether they take place in a register office, a church or some other licensed building, and there are four ways to be legally recognised as wife and husband (the contact details for all of them are listed in Chapter 12).

CIVIL CEREMONIES

At your local register office
The most straightforward way to get married in the UK is to go direct to your local register office.

What to do
Regardless of where you live, you need to get in touch with the superintendent registrar of the district where you wish to marry. Check your phone book under Registration of Births, Deaths and Marriages or get the central number from Chapter 12.

You must also give notice in person to your local superintendent registrar(s) at the register office in the district or districts where you both live. You can go to the office together if you both live in the same district but if you live in different registration districts each of you must give notice in your own district.

What you will need
A notice of marriage is a legal document and contains the following information:

* the names of the parties to the marriage;
* age;
* marital status;

- address;
- occupation;
- nationality; and
- intended venue for the marriage.

You will both need to prove that all the statements you have made are true and the best way to do this is to take your passports. Otherwise you'll each need two separate documents, such as a cheque book, cheque guarantee card, store/credit card or a birth certificate. Check this with the superintendent registrar before you go.

If you have been previously married, you need to produce a divorce decree absolute with the court's original stamp, or the death certificate of your former husband or wife.

You may be asked to produce other documents and your local superintendent registrar will tell you what you need. All your documents should be originals – photocopies aren't usually acceptable.

How long it takes
You both need to be living in England or Wales for at least seven days immediately before giving notice at the register office. After giving notice you must wait sixteen days before getting married.

What it costs
Fee for the superintendent registrar's certificates £60.00
Fee for the registrar to conduct the ceremony   £34.00
Fee for a marriage certificate on the wedding day   £3.50

You may be able to add some touches of your own, such as readings, to the civil wedding ceremony, as long as they aren't religious. You may even be allowed to take a video. However, this is all at the discretion of the superintendent registrar, and if you want to personalise your register office wedding you must check with them first.

In a building registered for weddings

There are lots of approved premises for weddings in England or Wales, including hotels, listed buildings and conference centres. If you'd like a civil wedding but you want it to be a bit more special than the local register office, you can get a list of the approved buildings in your area from your local authority or the Office of National Statistics. The list costs about £5 and it's regularly updated, but if you happen to spot somewhere that looks like the perfect place you can ask directly if they are licensed for weddings.

What to do

Choose your venue, either from the list of approved buildings or by looking around and choosing one you like and checking that it's approved by the local authority. Contact the venue and make your arrangements with them directly.

Give formal notice of your marriage to the superintendent registrar of the district(s) where you live. It doesn't matter whether the venue is in your local district or not, you still need to give notice to your own area superintendent registrar.

What you will need

Proof of your name, age, marital status, address, occupation, nationality and the place where you are getting married – exactly the same paperwork as if you were getting married in a register office.

How long it takes

If you pick a particularly popular venue, bear in mind that it may take longer to arrange your wedding than if you opted for a register office ceremony. Otherwise, the seven days residence qualification and sixteen days delay after giving notice are the same as for a register office wedding.

What it costs

The fee for the superintendent registrar's certificates is £60.00. The fee for the registrar to come to your venue and conduct the ceremony will vary according to the local authority, as will the fee for use of the venue. The fee for the marriage certificate is £3.50.

CHURCH OF ENGLAND WEDDINGS

If you want a religious wedding, getting married in the Church of England (or Church in Wales) is almost as simple as going to the register office because the Church of England is still the state-recognised church in the UK.

What to do

Call the vicar of the church in which you'd like to get married and arrange an appointment to go and see him or her. You don't even need to contact the superintendent registrar. The vicar can do that for you. All the legal and practical details are taken care of at the same time.

If you aren't a regular church-goer, you can find out the name and phone number of the priest (or at least the parish office) by looking at the church noticeboard.

What you will need
One of the couple needs to be a member of the Church of England and should live in the parish where the couple want to be married. It's best to have a clean slate as far as marriage is concerned if you want a Church of England wedding. The church doesn't allow remarriage in church of people who have been divorced, but individual priests may agree to it. Most priests will agree to give a blessing to a couple where one or both are divorced and have remarried in a civil ceremony. There is some flexibility on this and the best way to find out what to do is to talk to the vicar at your local church or the vicar of the church where you'd like to be married.

The usual proof of your name, age, marital status, address, occupation and nationality is required.

How long it takes
Some priests insist that a couple attend pre-marriage classes before the wedding and the classes may run over several months. Otherwise it depends on whether the marriage is by publication of banns or by special licence.

Publication of banns
The banns are read aloud in the church on three successive Sundays before the wedding and, if the couple live in different parishes, the banns must be read in both. You need to be resident in the parish for seven nights before the first Sunday of reading the banns right through to the last

Sunday (a minimum of 22 nights) and the wedding must take place within three months of the banns being read. The banns were originally a means of publicising the wedding to make sure no one had any objections, so if you are known by any name other than the one on your birth certificate you should give that one as well.

There is a small fee for reading the banns but, if one of you is divorced, it's the only way you can be married in the Church of England.

Common licence

This is quicker than reading the banns since only a day's notice is needed before the licence is issued. However, one of you needs to be living in the parish for at least 15 days before the wedding. Go to the priest at the chosen church to find out where to get the licence.

Special licence

These can only be issued by authority of the Archbishop of Canterbury from the Registrar of the Court of Faculties (see Chapter 12), and there has to be a special reason for it. Once granted, you can get married at any time in the church you have chosen, regardless of where you live.

What it costs

There is an overall fee, which includes all the necessary legal registration and certificates. The fees are set annually by the church. Currently, publication of the banns costs £16.00, the marriage service is £152.00 and the certificate of marriage £3.50. It is best to check what the fees will be for your own particular circumstances – see Chapter 12 for details of how to contact the Church of England.

There may be other fees involved – for the organist, bell ringers and choir for example – but they are unlikely to be very high.

A RELIGIOUS CEREMONY OTHER THAN THE CHURCH OF ENGLAND OR CHURCH IN WALES

You may want your wedding to be Buddhist, Catholic, Greek Orthodox, Hindu, Jewish, Muslim, non-conformist Christian, Sikh or some other religious tradition. If you do, the chances are that it's because you are already a member of that religious community and will have all the contacts you need to make the necessary arrangements. But if you've lapsed or drifted away and still want to get married in a religious setting, you'll need to start from scratch, contacting both the register office and the religious organisation to make the arrangements.

In Chapter 12 there is a list of contacts for a number of different religious groups. If the one you have chosen is not included, you'll be able to find a contact number in the telephone directory or on the Internet.

What to do

Contact either the religious organisation or the church or temple directly. They will be able to tell you whether or not you qualify to be married within the rules of their religion and help you make the arrangements. Check that the building is registered for marriages. Jewish weddings are the exception to the rule about registered buildings and can take place anywhere – even in the open air.

You also need to give the usual formal notice of your marriage to the superintendent registrar of the district(s) where you live. The superintendent registrar or some other authorised person (ask the registrar about this) must be present at the wedding to register the marriage.

What you will need

For the superintendent registrar you need the standard proof of your name, age, marital status, address, occupation, nationality and the place where you are getting married. For the religious organisation you may need proof of your religious background and affiliation. If you are getting married in a Catholic church you will need proof of baptism and confirmation.

How long it takes

Apart from the seven days' residence and sixteen days' gap after giving notice to the superintendent registrar, there may be a requirement for you to attend the church or temple on a regular basis or take marriage preparation classes. A Catholic priest, for example, will require up to six months' notice of your wedding and many Catholic churches prefer it to be longer. They see this as an essential time for preparation before making such a big commitment.

Religious weddings generally take longer to arrange than civil ones.

What it costs

Fee for the superintendent registrar's certificates £60.00

Fee for the registrar to conduct the ceremony   £40.00 (unless an 'authorised person' appointed by the trustees of the building has agreed to register the marriage)

Fee for a marriage certificate on the wedding day £3.50

There may be additional fees charged by the trustees of the building for the wedding, as well as by the person who performs the ceremony.

NON-RELIGIOUS WEDDINGS

A register office wedding is non-religious, of course, but if you want something a bit more ceremonial the Humanist Society will conduct weddings in any style you like and will even marry same-sex couples. Humanist weddings aren't legally recognised though, so, if you really want it to stick, you'll have to go to the register office as well.

LEGAL REQUIREMENTS FOR MARRIAGE IN THE UK

Age

The couple must both be over sixteen, and anyone under eighteen must have written consent from his or her parents or guardians.

Relationships

You cannot marry the following members of your own family:

- parent or adoptive parent
- grandparent
- child
- grandchild
- sibling
- aunt or uncle
- niece or nephew.

There are some restrictions about marrying step-relations and in-laws and it's best to check with your superintendent registrar if you are in any way related to your intended spouse.

Time

Weddings must be conducted between 8 a.m. and 6 p.m. Before electric lights were invented this was in order to ensure that no inferior substitutes were made for either the bride or the groom and that both parties could clearly see what they were getting. Jewish and Quaker ceremonies and weddings by special licence and registrar general's licence are the exception to this rule.

Place

Besides being registered for weddings, the venue must be public – the doors cannot be locked during the ceremony.

Paperwork

All the relevant certificates must be produced and handed to the official in charge of the ceremony before it begins.

Witnesses

Two witnesses are required at all weddings but they don't have to be known either to each other or to the couple getting married.

Validity

The wedding is invalid if:

♦ the bride and groom are not female and male by birth;

♦ one of them is already married and has not obtained a decree absolute of divorce;

- one of them is not of sound mind and does not understand what he or she is doing;

- one of them is under-age.

Names

Women don't have to change their names – it's a personal decision. But if you do decide to use your husband's name, remember to change your bank accounts, driving licence, income tax registration, DHSS, NHS and, most important, your passport. If you need your passport for your honeymoon, you can get a post-dated passport in your new name – just make sure you get the forms from the post office in plenty of time.

GETTING MARRIED ABROAD

If you decide to get married abroad, it's important to check that you are getting married legally and that the marriage will be recognised as legal when you return to the UK. There are organisations (usually holiday companies) who specialise in arranging foreign weddings and who will advise you about all this (see Chapter 12).

It's possible to register your wedding documents in the UK on your return and your local register office will be able to give you more details about this.

What to do

Contact a specialist holiday company, or book into a resort that specialises in weddings (Sandals, for example). If you want to arrange it yourself, first call the tourist board or the UK embassy of the country where you'd like to get married and find out exactly how to go about it.

What you will need

Check residence qualifications; and check what documentation you need (always a passport, but you may have to take your birth certificate, decree absolute (if relevant) and other documents).

How long it takes

In most of the popular wedding venues such as Las Vegas and the Caribbean, the lead-time is very short, but you may have to register your intention to marry and book a date some weeks in advance. Check this out as soon as you have decided a date, otherwise you may find you have a wasted trip.

What it costs

The cost of the actual wedding is usually very small compared to the cost of transporting yourself and your partner to your chosen exotic location and staying there for the required length of time. You may well save money on the cost of a reception in the UK, but you'll probably spend quite a lot on the wedding trip. However, if it doubles up as a honeymoon as well, in the end it may still be the cheapest option.

Expect respect and be respectful.

GETTING MARRIED: A REALITY CHECKLIST

☐ There are three parts to any wedding:

- ◆ The legal side of it.
- ◆ The personal emotional significance for the two of you.
- ◆ The ceremony – involving your family and friends.

For some people, all that matters is how they feel about each other and being legally married might seem irrelevant. For others, particularly in certain cultural settings, it's the family ceremony that's most significant, marking their move from one stage of life to another. It's a good idea to ask yourself which of those three matters most to you – or are they all equally important?

☐ Once you've answered the question for yourself, you need to talk this through with your partner. You may both be taking the wedding format for granted without realising that you each have something completely different in mind. Before you start fixing the arrangements you'll need to agree about what makes a marriage.

9

Invitations, Speeches and Thank-you Letters

You can buy ready-printed wedding invitations and even, if you look hard enough, ready-printed pre-invitations. There are plenty of books of wedding speeches which you can memorise or read once you've inserted the names of the people in your party. And, sadly, you can also buy pre-printed thank-you cards. So, in theory, you don't need a chapter on what to put in your invitations, speeches and thank-you letters − unless of course, you want them to be personal, meaningful and straight from the heart. Isn't that what weddings are all about?

INVITATIONS

Pre-invitations (PIs)

These are the notes you send to the people you *have* to invite to the wedding and they should go out at least a month *before* the formal invitations. It's a polite way of finding out how many of the 'duty' invitations actually have to be sent and saves having to resort to a reserve list. It also means that, when spaces are limited, you can minimise the places allocated to distant family members you don't really know. And that means you can free up more invitations for your friends.

It also cuts back on the 'no shows', which will help your budget. Even if spaces aren't restricted it's annoying to pay £50 a head for people who don't turn up on the day. If people get a PI first, followed by a real invitation a few weeks later, they are likely to get the message that your wedding invitations are to be taken seriously!

You can give a PI verbally but it's best to send out handwritten notes or personal emails. The message should be very clear:

> *If you don't let us know in the next four weeks whether you will be able to accept our wedding invitation, we won't actually be sending you one.*

What you actually write should be something like this:

> *I'm writing to let you know that David and I are getting married in Hamilton on 1 March at 2 o'clock with a reception to follow at the George Hotel. We'd love you to be there but as we only have space for a limited*

number of guests at the reception, I wonder if you could let me know if you're likely to be able to make it?[1]

Could you call/write/email me before 30 November and, if you are able to come, we will send you a formal invitation in about six weeks.

Formal invitations to the wedding

The usual wording is in the third person and the reply should be written in the same style (see Figure 1).

Mr and Mrs Joe Bloggs
request the pleasure of the company of

. . . .

at the marriage of their daughter
Josephine Maria
To
Mr David Smith
at St Mary's Church
Park Street
on Saturday 1 March
At 3.00 p.m.
and afterwards at a reception at
The George Hotel,
Park Street

RSVP
20 River Street
Hamilton
HL11 2NZ
07900 244443

Fig. 1. A formal invitation.

[1] You can put an extra paragraph for people you're really hoping to deter. Something like this should do this trick: 'We realise it's a long way for you to travel/the weather may not be so good at that time of year/accommodation is limited but I'm sure you could share a room with somebody...'.

Formal invitations to the evening party

A formal invitation to an evening party is given in Figure 2.

Mr and Mrs Joe Bloggs
request the pleasure of the company of
. . . .
at an Evening Reception
to be held at
The George Hotel, Park Street
On Saturday 1 March
At 8.30 p.m.
to celebrate the marriage of their daughter
Josephine Maria
to Mr David Smith

RSVP
20 River Street
Hamilton
HL11 2NZ
07900 244443

Fig. 2. Formal invitation to an evening party.

Formal reply

A formal reply is given in Figure 3.

Mr and Mrs John Jones thank Mr and Mrs Bloggs
for their kind invitation to their daughter's wedding and
reception and will be most happy to attend.

Fig. 3. A formal reply.

These examples are as formal as it gets, and you can de-formalise them as much as you want. Take a look around at different wording styles in the stationery catalogues and see what you feel comfortable with.

Informal invitations

If you're hosting your own wedding, getting married for the second time, or you just prefer to be informal, you might go for something more like Figure 4.

Josephine Bloggs and David Smith invite you to their wedding at St Mary's Church, Park Street on Saturday 1 March at 3.00 p.m. and afterwards at a reception at The George Hotel, Park Street

RSVP
20 River Street
Hamilton
HL11 2NZ
07900 244443

Fig. 4. An informal invitation.

Wedding stationery

If you decide to have your invitations printed, you might think about ordering any other wedding stationery you need at the same time. That way you can have your service or ceremony sheets, place cards or cake boxes all in your chosen style.

And your style, of course, can be anything you like. Wedding stationery always used to be silver and white but now it's pretty much any combination of colours, trimmed with ribbons, glitter, feathers and anything else you fancy.

Essential information

Whatever the style of invitation and however grand or simple the wedding, there is some essential information you need to include:

- Details of what you plan to provide at the reception or evening reception – a formal meal, hot or cold buffet or just canapés and drinks

- If there is to be dancing or any other entertainment (this is where you tell them if they need salsa lessons or invite them to bring their trombone and take part in the cabaret).

- What to wear (only if it's something unusual or you expect everybody to be in morning dress).

- Details of accommodation with phone numbers, websites and prices.

- A map.

- Flight information if you're getting married abroad.

You may already have sent out your PIs so that the real invitations will only be going out to people who are likely to accept. But, regardless of whether you think someone is actually coming to the wedding or not, you'll save yourself a lot of time and trouble if you include essential information with the invitation. For some people, knowing the distance involved and the options for accommodation may even affect their decision as to whether or not they accept.

TEN TOP TIPS FOR GREAT WEDDING SPEECHES

A bridegroom once told me he'd been so worried about his speech that he couldn't even remember making his wedding vows. If you're reading this, the chances are that you're one of the designated speechmakers for an upcoming wedding. The chances are also that you're a tiny little bit concerned about it – which is hardly surprising because, apparently, one of the commonest phobias is the fear of public speaking.

So here are the ten top tips for wedding speeches. If you take note of them, I can guarantee that, when the wedding day dawns and you hear another member of the wedding team jittering about his or her speech, you're going to smile to yourself and wonder what all the fuss was about. And then, you're going to forget all about it and enjoy the day.

At a wedding some years ago, the father of the bride was literally shaking with fear when the best man called on him to speak and, as he stood up, he dropped his meticulous notes all over the floor. The bride's uncle, sensing disaster, walked up to the top table and filled the gap with a few, off-the-cuff, heartfelt sentences about how much everybody loved the bride and liked her new husband and what a happy day it had been. By the time he'd finished, the bride's father, realising the heat was off, had regained his composure. Abandoning his notes, he walked over to join his brother and thanked him for stepping into the breach. 'You see,' he said, turning to the wedding party, 'that's what families are all about, and I'd like to welcome David (the bridegroom) into ours.' There was not a dry eye in the room.

Tip number 1: don't do it
Let's take the pressure off straight away. Admit to yourself, right now, that you don't have to make a speech. There is no law that says bridegrooms, best men and

bride's fathers have to turn into stand-up comics on a day when they've got much more important things to think about.

And remember, you aren't just making this decision for your own benefit – there is nothing in the world more miserable than watching somebody trying to make a speech when he or she doesn't want to. If you're a reluctant orator, you can make a whole roomful of people happy simply by not making them listen to you! In fact, you'll be doing everybody a favour.

Look at it like this: you wouldn't normally attempt to do something you weren't qualified for, would you? Unless you happen to be a professional confectioner you probably wouldn't volunteer to ice the wedding cake, and if you aren't in the couture business you wouldn't offer to make the wedding dress. Speeches are no different: if you don't usually make them, this is not the time to experiment. It's not fair on the bride and groom or the rest of the guests.

Tip number 2: use the 'no speech kit'

Write down the few words that you do have to say on a piece of card and practise reading them out loud a few times (the 'no speech kit' – see Figure 5).

Tip number 3: appoint a deputy

For every ten people who are terrified of public speaking, there's one who loves it and the chances are that, if you've got more than ten people on your side of the family, there will be one at least who is quite comfortable with standing

---

Bride's father
I'd like to welcome you all to my daughter's wedding and ask you please to stand up and join me in a toast to the bride and groom.

Bridegroom
Thank you all for being here today to share this special day with (bride's name) and me. I'd also like to thank my new parents-in-law, (names), for all their hard work in making it such a wonderful occasion, and my parents too for all their help and support. And now will you please join in a toast to the beautiful bridesmaids, (names).

Best man
On behalf of (bridesmaid's names), I'd like to thank you for those kind words. And now I'd like to read some messages from some of your friends who couldn't be here today but who want you both to know that they are thinking of you. (reads cards and messages).

Feel free to add any extra thanks and compliments if you feel confident enough and you can remember the right people's names.

Fig. 5. The 'no speech kit'.

up and telling a few jokes on your behalf. There's no need to apologise or justify sending in a substitute, just deliver your 'no speech kit' and then say 'and now, my brother-in-law/friend/cousin/aunt/wife would like to say a few words'. When the substitute has finished, the best man simply introduces the next speaker.

Tip number 4: do a team talk
If the bride's father, bridegroom and best man all happen to be reluctant public speakers, you could always do a team talk. Being in the limelight isn't half so scary if

you're sharing it with two other people. Agree in advance about who will speak first, stand up together and share the announcements and toasts. Speak as if you're talking to each other and the audience are simply listening in. You've heard this done many times if you've ever listened to DJs chatting on breakfast radio. They get the information about the latest competition or special offer across by talking about it rather than announcing it. You have to fit in the specific toasts and thank-yous, of course, but basically you're having a little chat about the wedding.

One of you will start by commenting about the meal perhaps – 'that was a lovely supper' and the others join in 'and doesn't the cake look fantastic,' then 'hasn't everybody done well...' You can tell a couple of stories about little things that *nearly* went wrong, perhaps, and then round off on a positive note with the toasts and votes of thanks.

Tip number 5: forget the speech and put on a show
Another alternative to the traditional wedding speech and one that usually works really well is to put on a show, using visual aids. Either one of you or all three can do this.

Borrow a projector of some kind (the reception venue may well have one and a screen as well but check this in advance) and prepare a set of funny, touching, relevant photos and even sketches or cartoons. They could be pictures of the bride and groom, respectively, looking cute as children, pictures of their parents' wedding (usually good for a laugh) and any family classics you may have in the album. The best man and bridesmaids may be able to contribute a few photos as well.

Write a few comments on separate cards about each photo and, while one of you puts up the pictures, the other two read the comments. I've seen this done many times, and it's always fun provided you stick to the golden rule: *no nudity* and *keep it clean*. It's meant to make people laugh, not cringe. It takes quite a bit of setting up and you'll need to get together to rehearse, but you'll probably enjoy it and so will your audience.

Tip number 6: make it a variety performance

If you're the best man, you can talk this through with the bridegroom and bride's father, but they're likely to approve of this idea because it takes a lot of pressure off the three of you and spreads it more evenly around the other guests. A few weeks before the wedding, get together with the bridegroom and bride's father and make a list of any guests you think might be willing to say a few words of tribute to the bride or groom, tell a joke or recite a poem. Contact them all and ask if they'd like to take part. If it's a fairly large wedding party, the chances are you'll get several willing volunteers. Check in advance what they are going to do and make sure it's suitable and then give them a batting order on the day.

Tip number 7: start with a story

If, after reading this far you are still planning to make a speech, it probably means you've done it before and are quite happy to do it again, in which case you don't need me to tell you what to say. But, just in case you do, here are a few more tips to make sure your speech will be a success.

Start with a story. Never start by saying you aren't used to making speeches or you feel nervous. Tell a story about the bride or groom, or both, or a story about something that happened in the wedding preparations – even a story about your own wedding. It doesn't matter, but remember this: the minute you start to tell a story, people start to listen and they'll go right on listening until the end because people are hooked on stories. That's why they watch soap operas.

A famous rule for writers is 'write about what you know' and this also applies to speeches. Instead of telling a joke you've memorised from a book, dip into your own experience and tell a story involving the key people at the wedding, preferably one in which you were actually involved. It doesn't have to be hilarious, and it should never be scandalous but it must be true. That way you don't have to worry about remembering the details or getting it in the right order – if you get muddled you can appeal for help from the other people who also remember it! Just a simple little story is all you need, and our lives are full of them. If you can't remember any off the top of your head, ask your partner and some other family members or take a look through the old photo albums. The memories will come flooding back.

I'll give you an example – you don't need a preamble, that's distracting. Just pitch right in to the story:

I remember when Jo was a little girl and I went to the parents' evening at the school.

Tip number 8: only tell half the story
Here's the next trick. Only tell half the story:

We all queued up to see the teachers and when it was my turn, I could see from the teacher's face that it wasn't good news. The first thing she said to me was, 'I'm sorry to say this, Mr Bloggs, but we've been having a few problems with Jo.' So I said to her, 'well, you'd better tell me what sort of problems you're having,' and that was when she told me what Jo had done on the nature walk.

Tip number 9: use your story to name names
I don't suppose you even remember that Jo, but your mother and I were so cross with you. And then we came home and told your granny about it and, believe it or not, she laughed! Your granny never could be tough on you, could she?

This is a great way of bringing in any people you want to remember, thank or congratulate – which of course, is the real purpose of your speech.

And just mentioning her name makes me think how proud and happy your granny would be if she could be here today. She was a very special person and I know Jo probably misses her more than anybody so, before I go on, I'd like to propose a toast to Jo's granny (pause for everybody to raise their glasses).

Oh, and before I forget, I really must say thank you to some other very wonderful people who are here today. Starting, of course, with Jo's mum for all her hard work in making this such a wonderful day. If Jo and David are as happy as Nicole and I have been for the past x years, they'll be very lucky indeed.

And, of course, this celebration wouldn't have been half as much fun if you hadn't all made the effort to be here with us, helping us celebrate. I know that some of you have come a very long way – especially Molly, the chief bridesmaid who's flown in all the way from Seattle just to walk up the aisle behind Jo today. These two girls have been friends ever since junior school of course and I've got a feeling that Molly might even have been involved in the nature walk incident as well.

Tip number 10: close the loop

Remember to save the end of your story for the very end of your speech. As long as the loop is open you will have your audience's attention. When you close it, you give them the sense of completion and they'll be relaxed and ready for the next speaker:

And for those of you who might be wondering what did happen on that nature walk, I might as well tell you that Jo had apparently filled the teacher's handbag with worms while she wasn't looking. She didn't discover it until they got back to the classroom. Well, Jo and Molly, I don't know how long it took you to collect enough worms to fill up a handbag, but looking at these two elegant young ladies standing here now, I think you will agree with me that it's hard to imagine them getting dirt under their fingernails.

But anyway, as I was saying, we are very happy to welcome you all to share this special day and I'd like to propose a toast to my beautiful daughter, Jo, and her bridegroom, David, who is a great guy. Of course, I'd rather she'd chosen somebody who didn't beat me at golf quite so easily, but you can't have everything.

THANK-YOU LETTERS

There is no substitute for just sitting down and writing them, personally, one at a time. If your presents are arriving in batches before the wedding and you've got time, you can start right away. But if you're too busy beforehand, you're probably going to find life a little quiet for a while afterwards, so you'll have plenty of time for letter writing.

◆ Motivate yourself to do it by making it a part of the wedding ritual. Light a few candles, play the wedding music and allow yourself to enjoy the memories.

◆ Minimise the actual writing. Apart from mentioning the specific present and saying something nice about it, you can make your letter interesting without writing very much at all. A picture paints a thousand words so, if there were disposable cameras at the wedding, you can include a few photos of the person you're writing to with a sprinkle of table confetti as well.

◆ Remember to include a typed slip explaining how they can view and order the official photographs if they want them. This should be tactfully worded so that they don't feel under pressure. If you are sending out pieces of cake, do it at the same time. That way you only have to look up the address once, even if you have to write it down twice.

♦ Involve your spouse. One of you can do the writing while the other one sorts out photographs and addresses the envelope. If you have all the addresses and a note of the presents on a PC you can even print out labels. It's fine to have typed envelopes as long as the letter is handwritten.

Take nothing for granted. Every day you wake up and find you're still together is worth celebrating.

INVITATIONS, SPEECHES AND THANK-YOU LETTERS CHECKLIST

☐ Avoid trying to be word perfect, either with your invitations, your speeches or your thank-you letters. Wedding words, like marriages, can be emotional, sincere, spontaneous and full of love. Perfection isn't possible, so stop trying.

☐ Invitations need to be clear, timely and a pleasure to receive and they should contain *all* the relevant information.

☐ Speeches should only be made by people who enjoy making them. It's better to write your speech on a flip chart and turn it over a page at a time to a musical accompaniment than to force yourself and your guests to suffer agonies of embarrassment on your behalf.

☐ Think of your thank-you letters as memory-sharing moments. Aim to share some of the joy of the wedding with both the guests who were there with you and the ones who couldn't make it but sent presents instead.

10

Wedding Words and Music

Your vows and readings should mean something special to you both so, if you can't find anything that sums up exactly what you feel, you could try writing them yourselves. Keeping them simple is the best way to put your feelings into your own words. Think carefully about whom you ask to do the readings: members of your wedding team or family members and friends? And, whatever music you decide on, if any of it's going to be performed live, make sure your musicians are happy about playing it.

WEDDING WORDS

Some of these words will be familiar to you and some of them won't. And there are plenty more to choose from. If you can't find quite what you want here, it's worth spending a day having a look on the Internet as well as in your local library and some of the bigger bookshops to find some unusual readings.

Vows

> I add my breath to your breath
> That our days may be long on the earth
> That the days of our people may be long
> That we may be one person
> That we may finish our roads together
> May our mother bless you with life
> May our paths be fulfilled
>
> *Keres Indian song*

You are my wife, my feet shall run because of you, my feet dance because of you, my heart shall beat because of you, my eyes see because of you, my mind thinks because of you, and I shall love because of you.

Eskimo marriage song

> From this day forward,
> You shall not walk alone,
> My heart will be your shelter,
> And my arms will be your home.
>
> *Anon*

I cannot promise you a life of sunshine;
I cannot promise riches, wealth, or gold;
I cannot promise you an easy pathway
That leads away from change or growing old.

But I can promise all my heart's devotion;
A smile to chase away your tears of sorrow;
A love that's ever true and ever growing;
A hand to hold in yours through each tomorrow.

Anon

This is a joy beyond all other joys – the day the dream I scarcely dared to dream comes true, all happiness is here and hope and certainty. Today we begin to shape a life – one greater than any we could have made alone.

Pam Brown

I take you now and for always, for always is always now.

Philip Larkin

I love you without how or when or from where; I love you simply without problems or pride; I love you in this way because I don't know any other way of living.

Pablo Neruda

We have taken the seven steps.
You have become mine forever.
Yes, we have become partners.
I have become yours.
Hereafter, I cannot live without you.
Do not live without me.
Let us share the joys.

We are word and meaning, united.
You are thought and I am sound.
May the nights be honey-sweet for us;
May the mornings be honey-sweet for us;
may the heavens be
honey-sweet for us.
May the plants be honey-sweet for us;
may the sun be all honey for us;
may the cows yield us
honey-sweet milk!
As the heavens are stable,
as the earth is stable,
as the mountains are stable,
as the whole universe is stable,
so may our union be
permanently settled.

Hindu marriage ceremony

It's all I have to bring today,
This, and my heart beside,
This, and my heart, and all the fields,
And all the meadows wide,
Be sure you count, should I forget, –
Some one the sun could tell, –
This and my heart, and all the bees
Which in the clover dwell.

Emily Dickinson

Before we met, you and I were halves unjoined except in
the wide rivers of our minds. We were each other's distant
shore, the opposite wings of a bird, the other half of a
seashell. We did not know the other then, did not know

our determination to keep alive the cry of one riverbank to the other. We were apart. Yet connected in our ignorance of each other, like two apples sharing a common tree. Remember? I knew you existed long before you understood my desire to join my freedom to yours. Our paths collided long enough for our indecision to be swallowed up by the greater need of love. When you came to me, the sun surged toward the earth and the moon escaped from darkness to bless the union of two spirits so alike that the Creator had designed them for life's endless circle. Beloved partner, keeper of my heart's odd secrets, clothed in summer blossoms so the icy hand of winter never touches us. I thank your patience. Our joining is like a tree to earth, a cloud to sky and even more. We are the reason the world can laugh on its battlefield and rise from the ashes of its selfishness to hear me say, in this time, this place, this way – I loved you best of all.

Commitment poem of the Pueblo Indian

Blessings
May your hands be forever clasped in friendship and your hearts joined forever in love.

Anonymous

> Let all thy joys be as the month of May,
> And all thy days be as a marriage day:
> Let sorrow, sickness and a troubled mind
> Be stranger to thee.

Francis Quarles

You shall be together even in the silent memory of God.
But let there be spaces in your togetherness, and let the
winds of the heavens dance between you.

The Prophet by Kahlil Gibran

Now you will feel no rain,
For each of you will be shelter to the other,
Now you will feel no cold,
For each of you will be warmth to the other,
Now there is no loneliness for you,
Now there is no more loneliness,
Now you are two persons
But there is one life before you.
Go now to your dwelling place
to enter into the days of your togetherness.

Apache wedding blessing

Here all seeking is over,
the lost has been found,
a mate has been found
to share the chills of winter –
now Love asks that you be united,
Here is a place to rest,
a place to sleep, a place in heaven,
the two are becoming one,
the black night is scattered,
the eastern sky grows bright.
At last the great day has come!

Hawaiian wedding song

Today the drab world has been transformed – decked out
with flowers and ribbons, a feat, a celebration, rich with

music and laughter, kind thoughts and recollections, all in their best – and you, figures from romance, all the world rejoices in a new beginning.

Pam Brown

There shall be such a oneness between you that when one weeps, the other shall taste salt.

Proverb

> But when two people are at one
> in their inmost hearts,
> they shatter even the strength of iron
> or bronze.
> And when two people understand each other
> in their inmost hearts,
> their words are sweet and strong
> like the fragrance of orchids.

I Ching

From the groom to the bride

This girl all in white
Is my crystal of light
Kissed by heaven to earth in a dancing gift
Of a bride in her freshness, whom youth and love lift,
With two sunbeams for bridesmaids, their
    father's delight.
I have married my bride
In a ring of green fields
Round a church on a hill where all nature's her
    dress...

From 'Epithalamium' by Francis Warner

My Luve is like a red, red rose,
That's newly sprung in June:
My Luve is like the melodie
That's sweetly play'd in tune.

As fair art thou, my bonie lass,
So deep in luve am I;
And I will luve thee still, my Dear,
Till a' the seas gang dry.

Till a' the seas gang dry, my Dear,
And the rocks melt wi' the sun:
I will luve thee still, my Dear,
While the sands o' life shall run.

And fare-thee well, my only luve!
And fare-thee well, a while!
And I will come again, my luve,
Tho' 't were ten thousand mile!

Robert Burns

You have intensified all colours, deepened all delight. I love you more than life, my beauty, my wonder.

Duff Cooper

From the bride to the groom

My true love hath my heart, and I have his
By just exchange one for the other given:
I hold his dear, and mine he cannot miss;
There never was a better bargain driven.
His heart in me keeps me and him in one;
My heart in him his thoughts and senses guides:
He loves my heart, for once it was his own;
I cherish his, because in me it bides.

His heart his wound received from my sight;
My heart was wounded with his wounded heart;
For, as from me on him his hurt did light,
So still me-thought in me his hurt did smart:
Both equal hurt in this change sought our bliss:
My true love hath my heart and I have his.

'The Bargain' by Sir Philip Sidney

From the bride or groom to each other

You and I
Have so much love
That it burns like fire
In which we baked a lump of clay
Moulded into a figure of you
And a figure of me.
Then we take both of them
And break them into pieces
And mix the pieces with water,
And mould again a figure of you
And a figure of me.
I am your clay,
In life we share a single quilt
In death we will share one coffin

Kuan Tao-Sheng

Though the sound overpowers,
Sing again, with your dear voice revealing
A tone
Of some world far from ours,
Where music and moonlight and feeling
Are one.

'To Jane: The Keen Stars were Twinkling'
by Percy Bysshe Shelley

You and I have floated here on the stream
That brings from the fount
At the heart of time love of one for another.
We have played alongside millions of lovers,
Shared in the same
Shy sweetness of meeting,
The same distressful tears of farewell –
Old love, but in shapes that renew and renew forever.
Today it is heaped at your feet, it had found its end in
    you,
The love of all man's days both past and forever:
Universal joy, universal sorrow, universal life,
The memories of all loves merging with this one
    love of ours –
And the songs of every poet past and forever.

Rabindranath Tagore

Readings

We looked into each other's eyes. I saw myself, she saw herself.

Stanislaw J. Lec

Love is a temporary madness, it erupts like volcanoes and then subsides. And when it subsides you have to make a decision. You have to work out whether your root was so entwined together that it is inconceivable that you should ever part. Because this is what love is. Love is not breathlessness, it is not excitement, it is not the promulgation of promises of eternal passion...that is just being in love, which any fool can do. Love itself is what is left over when being in love has burned away, and this is both an art and a fortunate accident. Those that truly love have roots that grow towards each other underground, and when all the pretty blossoms have fallen from their branches, they find that they are one tree and not two.

from: 'Captain Corelli's Mandolin' by Louis de Bernières

Let me not to the marriage of true minds
Admit impediments. Love is not love
Which alters when it alteration finds,
Or bends with the remover to remove:
O, no! it is an ever-fixed mark,
That looks on tempests and is never shaken;
It is the star to ever wand'ring bark,
Whose worth's unknown, although his height be taken.
Love's not Time's fool, though rosy lips and cheeks
Within his bending sickle's compass come;
Love alters not with his brief hours and weeks,
But bears it out even to the edge of doom.
If this be error, and upon me prov'd,
I never writ, nor no man ever lov'd.

Sonnet 116 by William Shakespeare

Nothing is sweeter than love, nothing stronger, nothing higher, nothing wider, nothing happier, nothing fuller, nothing better in heaven and earth.

'Love Divine' by Thomas A. Kempis

You can give without loving, but you can never love without giving. The great acts of love are done by those who are habitually performing small acts of kindness. We pardon to the extent that we love. Love is knowing that even when you are alone, you will never be lonely again.

And the great happiness of life is the conviction that we are loved. Loved for ourselves. And even loved in spite of ourselves.

'Les Miserables' by Victor Hugo

Today is a day you will always remember – the greatest
   in anyone's life.
You'll start off the day just two people in love
And end it as husband and wife.

It's a brand new beginning, the start of a journey
With moments to cherish and treasure.
And although there'll be times when you both disagree,
These will surely be outweighed by pleasure.
You'll have heard many words of advice in the past
When the secrets of marriage were spoken,
But you know that the answers lie hidden inside
Where the bond of true love lies unbroken.

So live happy for ever as lovers and friends
It's the dawn of a new life for you
As you stand there together with love in your eyes
From the moment you whisper 'I do'.

And with luck, all your hopes, and your dreams can
   be real,
May success find its way to your hearts.
Tomorrow can bring you the greatest of joys
But today is the day it all starts.

Anon

One-liners

Love has nothing to do with what you are expecting to get – only with what you are expecting to give – which is everything.

Katharine Hepburn

Nobody has ever measured, not even poets, how much the heart can hold.

Zelda Fitzgerald

Love is a canvas furnished by nature and embroidered by imagination.

Voltaire

For it was not into my ear you whispered, but into my heart. It was not my lips you kissed, but my soul.

Judy Garland

Bible passages: some of the favourites

Genesis 1: 26–31
The story of creation where God makes man and woman in his own image.

Ecclesiastes 3: 1–15
'A time to be born and a time to die...'
The passage that acknowledges the rhythms of life, including marriage.

Ecclesiastes 4: 9–12
'Two are better than one' and 'A cord of three strands is not easily broken', which means the marriage that includes God is stronger than a contract made between two people alone.

Ruth 1: 1–17
A story about loyalty and love which contains the promise 'wherever you go, I will go – your people shall be my people'.

Song of Solomon 4: 10–11
Some lovely, and not particularly religious, words from bridegroom to bride.

Mark 10: 6–16
Jesus' teachings about marriage and children.

John 15: 1–13
'Love bears all things, believes all things, hopes all things, endures all things. Love never fails and now abide faith, hope, love, these three; but the greatest of these is love.'

1 John 4: 7–21
'Beloved, let us love one another, for love is of God' and 'perfect love casts out fear'.

WEDDING MUSIC

Some wedding music is so traditional that, even if you aren't a fan of classical music, you can recognise it as soon as you hear it. The advantage of choosing something so familiar, especially for a church wedding, is that it helps the guests to get into the right mood very quickly and it also gives them some useful cues as to what is likely to happen next.

Music to play while the guests are arriving
Air from the *Water Music* (Handel)

Canon in D (Pachelbel)

Air on a G String (Bach)

Ave Verum Corpus (Bach)

Chanson de Matin (Elgar)

Largo from *Xerxes* (Handel)

Minuet (Boccherini)

Music for the bride

Arrival of the Queen of Sheba (Handel)

Bridal March from *Lohengrin* (Here comes the bride) (Wagner)

Grand march from *Aida* (Verdi)

The Wedding March (Mendelssohn)

Hornpipe from the *Water Music* (Handel)

Salut D'amour (Elgar)

Wedding March from *The Marriage of Figaro* (Mozart)

Signing the register

Ave Maria (Schubert)

Jesu, Joy of Man's Desiring (Bach)

Arioso (Bach)

The Call (Vaughan Williams)

Let the Bright Seraphim (Handel)

Panis Angelicus (Franck)

Music for the bride and groom as they leave the ceremony

Trumpet Voluntary (Jeremiah Clark)

Toccata (Symphony No 5) (Widor)

Music for the Royal Fireworks (Handel)

Brandenburg Concerto No 3 (Bach)

Coronation March (Walton)

Ode to Joy (Symphony No. 9) (Beethoven)

Trumpet Tune in C (Purcell)

Wedding March from *A Midsummer Night's Dream* (Mendelssohn)

Hymns for a church wedding

Although not specifically wedding hymns, these are all popular choices for weddings:

All Creatures of our God and King
All People that on Earth do Dwell
All Things Bright and Beautiful
As I Kneel Before You
Blest Be the Tie that Binds
Colours of Day
Come Down, oh Love Divine
Dear Lord and Father of Mankind
Oh God, whose Loving Hand has Led thy Children to this Joyful Day
The King of Love my Shepherd is
Lead us, Heavenly Father, Lead us
The Lord is my Shepherd
Lord of all Hopefulness
Lord of the Dance
Love Divine, all Loves Excelling
Morning has Broken
Oh Perfect Love
Praise my Soul, the King of Heaven
Praise to the Lord, the Almighty, the King of Creation
Shine, Jesus, Shine
Walk with Me, oh my Lord

WORDS AND MUSIC CHECKLIST

☐ It's lovely to have vows and readings that mean something special to you both. If you can't find anything that sums up exactly what you feel, how about writing it yourselves? You don't have to be a poet: keep it simple and see if you can put your feelings into words.

☐ Whether you write your own words or use Shakespeare's, you might like to consider getting them framed or even putting them in the front of your wedding album. You can get a calligrapher to copy them, or type them up on your PC and print them out in an elegant font.

☐ Think about whom you would like to do the readings. You could ask members of your wedding team or you could make it a way of involving other family members and friends.

☐ You can buy plenty of recordings of wedding music to help you make your final selection. If any of it's going to be performed live, make sure your musicians are happy about playing whatever you've chosen and that it's within their normal repertoire.

11

The Countdown
to your Wedding

It's a good idea to be relaxed about your wedding arrangements: it puts less of a strain on your relationship with your partner and gives you a better chance of enjoying your special celebration together. But there's a difference between being relaxed and being disorganised. You need, therefore, to create a checklist or countdown to your wedding that lists all the necessary items you will need and that keeps track of all the major events leading up to your wedding day.

A particularly laid-back bride and bridegroom recently celebrated their wedding a week before it happened. Knowing that their chosen reception venue was extremely popular, they booked it 18 months ahead of time. They also sorted out the wedding dress, the cake and the photographer well in advance. Six months before the wedding date, they called at the church where they wanted to get married and discovered that funds had finally been raised to replace the roof. The work was due to finish the day before the wedding and the vicar, who was sceptical about the builders' timing, refused to accept their booking until the week *after* the reception.

SIX GOOD REASONS FOR STARTING YOUR COUNTDOWN NOW

1. You can't keep it all in your head and you can't be prepared to every eventuality. And whether it's a major item like the wedding ceremony or a minor one like the bridesmaids' gifts that go astray, it's bound to be stressful. But you'll have a better chance of giving yourself the planning time you need if you have a countdown checklist.

2. Working out a countdown with your partner is often a good memory jogger – as you go through your deadlines from now to your wedding day you'll find you think of lots of little details you might otherwise have neglected.

3. Your countdown will be even more useful if you update it as you go along. Things will change, deadlines will shift and you'll think of things that hadn't occurred to you before.

4. It's also an insurance policy. If you want to rely on your memory, that's fine – but if you have a wedding support team (your best man, bridesmaids, mother and mother-in-law to be, for example) you can given them all a copy of the countdown. It saves you having to remind them about what they're supposed to do all the time, and you might find they help to keep you on schedule as well.

5. You can make your own version of this list and put it in your diary – you can even get very special and very glamorous wedding diaries for this. Or you download it all into your personal organiser or PC.

6. As your wedding day gets nearer, you might like to print out a copy of the list and post it up somewhere so that you (and your support team) can keep track of everything.

Note: A simplified version of the following can be found on page 187, which you might like to use as your own personal checklist.

AS SOON AS YOU DECIDE TO GET MARRIED

Set a provisional date for the wedding and tell all the important people in your life about it. Make the basic decisions about what sort of ceremony you want:

♦ A religious ceremony or a civil one?

♦ If it's a civil wedding, do you want to have it in a register office or a licensed venue?

♦ If you go for a licensed venue, which one do you want it to be?

Get in touch with the appropriate people about your ceremony:

♦ provisionally book the register office;

♦ find out how much notice the superintendent registrar will need to attend a licensed venue; or

♦ contact your chosen religious organisation.

Check the legal requirements for your type of wedding ceremony, including:

♦ residency; and

♦ documents (birth certificate, decree absolute certificate, etc.).

Start talking to anyone other than the two of you who might want to help pay for the wedding – your parents, for example. Make a tentative guest list – this has a bearing on the kind of venue you choose and it will affect your budget. Agree on the budget. Check out the reception venue you want (unless it's the same as the venue for the ceremony). Some reception venues are booked years in advance, especially for Saturdays in summer. Think about whether you want to arrange it all yourself or whether you'd like a wedding co-ordinator (this is an expensive option).

Plan your honeymoon – if you're going abroad you can often get much cheaper deals by booking well in advance.

Provisionally book your first-night hotel room or bridal suite. Take out wedding insurance before you pay any deposits. Suppliers and even venues sometimes let you down, and finding last-minute replacements can be expensive.

The bride's checklist

☐ Start reading magazines and looking at websites to give you ideas about your ceremony, your reception and, of course, the dress!

☐ Start a file on everything from your shoes to the cake and cut out articles and pictures that you like.

☐ Focus on your wedding dress and think about what you want. Make some appointments to start trying them on – most manufacturers change their styles twice a year.

SIX MONTHS BEFORE

Send out your pre-invitations. By now, if you haven't done so already, you should be confirming all your major arrangements:

- ◆ The ceremony.
- ◆ The venue and catering.
- ◆ The honeymoon and first-night booking.

Book your photographer – and arrange for a video if you want one. Make sure you are very clear about what the deal is, how many shots he or she will take, how many you get to choose from and how many you get to keep. Will you get a set of proofs to send round to your guests? Or can they be posted up on the Internet?

Order the cake. Do some research and hire the entertainment for the reception. The best bands and discos get booked up a long way ahead, especially at weekends.

Choose, inspect and hire your wedding transport. Make sure you see the actual vehicles – photographs can be misleading. If you're planning something unusual, check whether it's practical. Huge wedding cars can't always get down small country lanes to quaint old churches.

Order the wedding stationery:

- Invitations.
- Order of ceremony sheets (confirm the details with the superintendent registrar or priest).
- Place cards.
- Wedding-cake boxes.
- Menus.

Choose your wedding support team:

- Best man.
- Bridesmaids, maids of honour, flower girls, pages.
- Ushers.

Think about what the men in the wedding party are going to wear and, if necessary, make arrangements to hire or buy their outfits.

Book the florist:

◆ Decorations and arrangements for the ceremony.
◆ Decorations and arrangements for the reception.
◆ Bouquets for bride and bridesmaids.
◆ Buttonholes.
◆ Corsages for female guests of honour.
◆ Bouquets for mothers and grannies.

Arrange crèche facilities, special meals and entertainment for small children. Choose your wedding rings. Put your wedding-gift list together.

If you're going abroad for your honeymoon, check your passports are valid and, if you're the bride, make a decision about whether you want to change your passport over to your husband's name.

The bride's checklist

☐ Choose your dress and your bridesmaids' dresses. Remember to allow time for alterations if these are shop-bought dresses or for fittings if you are having them made.

☐ Begin your pre-wedding beauty routine.

☐ Start exercising if you need to get into shape. Taking time out for yourself to exercise will also help you stay relaxed over the next six months.

☐ Promise yourself that you'll eat healthy food from now on (plenty of fresh fruit and vegetables) and that you'll drink plenty of water. This will help you feel good as well as making sure your hair and skin are looking good.

☐ Experiment with your hair and make-up. If you want to try out a new colour, give it a trial run – you still have time to grow it out if you don't like it.

THREE MONTHS BEFORE

Call the first meeting of your wedding support team. Draw up your final guest list, based on the responses to your pre-invitations. Send out the invitations, remembering to include directions and accommodation details. Have the wedding list ready for the people who request it.

Decide on the wedding menu and wine. Confirm:

◆ The wedding-cake design.

◆ The music for the venue and decide what to do about the first dance.

◆ The details of your wedding ceremony. If you haven't already done it when you ordered your printed order of ceremonies, now is the time to make the final decision on music and readings.

◆ The flowers you will need. Make sure that female guests (mothers and grannies) are happy with the colours you've chosen for their corsages.

If you are having a register office wedding, you should confirm it by now. Finalise your honeymoon plans and find out about vaccinations and visas. Check that the male members of the wedding team, including the bridegroom, have their suits and accessories organised.

The bride's checklist

☐ Discuss hair styles with your hairdresser. Take along any veil or head dress that you are interested in, a picture of your dress if possible and an idea of your colour scheme.

☐ Arrange for a trial run for your make-up. Take along a picture of your dress and an idea of your colour scheme and flowers. Ask someone to take plenty of photographs of your suggested hair and make-up so you can get an idea of what you will look like in your wedding pictures and adjust the styles accordingly.

☐ Buy shoes and accessories for yourself and your bridesmaids.

☐ Buy your going-away outfit.

☐ Liaise with both mothers on their choices of outfits and colours.

TWO MONTHS BEFORE

This is the time for the best man and chief bridesmaid to arrange the stag night and hen party. Send out wedding-present lists to anyone who requests them. Start a list of the wedding gifts you receive and mark up the ones who have already had thank-you letters. Make sure all the guests have somewhere to stay and book accommodation for them if necessary.

Buy any little bits and pieces you might want for your reception:

◆ A guest book for people to sign on your wedding day.

◆ Table decorations, candles and almonds or small gifts for the guests.

◆ Disposable cameras.

Write the speeches and practise them.

The bride's checklist

☐ If you're planning to use your husband's name at all, now is the time to start informing banks, credit card companies, employers, doctor and dentist.

☐ Buy gifts for the bridesmaids and your fiancé.

☐ Liaise with your fiancé to buy gifts for the best man and ushers.

ONE MONTH BEFORE

Call a meeting of the wedding support team. Chase up any guests who haven't replied to their invitations. Let the reception venue and caterers know the final numbers. Check that the outfits for the wedding party are all organised. At the same time and day of the week as the wedding, arrange to have a practice run from the bride's house to the wedding venue. Draw up your table plan. The order of ceremony sheets, menus and place cards should have been delivered.

The bride's checklist
Make the personal appointments you'll need for yourself and your bridesmaids:

☐ hair
☐ make-up
☐ manicure and pedicure.

Start your tanning sessions if you're planning to have them. Collect your dress. Is your wedding outfit complete?

☐ Underwear?
☐ Shoes?
☐ Veil and head dress?
☐ Something old, new, borrowed and blue?
☐ Flowers?
☐ Jewellery?

Are the bridesmaids' outfits complete? Have you bought your going-away outfit and honeymoon clothes?

TWO WEEKS BEFORE
Confirm everything:

- ceremony
- reception
- cake
- flowers

- transport
- honeymoon and first-night accommodation.

Order your foreign currency for the honeymoon.

Make a list of telephone numbers in case of an emergency on the day:

- a local cab firm;
- all the suppliers; and
- key people (especially mobile numbers).

The bride's checklist
You should try to do the following:

☐ Wear your wedding shoes around the house. You can put socks over them if you really want to protect them.

☐ Step up the beauty routine.

ONE WEEK BEFORE
Call the final pre-wedding meeting of the support team and check that:

- everyone knows what he or she is doing;

- everyone's got everything he or she needs;

- somebody's going to collect the wedding presents after the reception; and

- somebody's going to return any outfits that have been hired.

Arrange the final rehearsal at the venue for the ceremony and also the rehearsal dinner, if you're having one.

Make sure you have as much help as you need immediately before the wedding. If you are decorating the ceremony and reception venues yourself, for example, you will need extra helpers. Your wedding support team will already be busy – and so will you!

The bride's checklist
☐ Make the final arrangements with your bridesmaids.

☐ Double-check your outfit.

THE DAY BEFORE
Check that the best man has the rings. Speak to the wedding support team on the phone if you're not going to be seeing them.

The bride's checklist
☐ Eat some breakfast – persuade someone to bring it to you in bed!

☐ Have your pedicure and manicure if you aren't having them on the morning.

☐ Pack your clothes for after the wedding and arrange for them to be taken to the reception or first-night hotel.

☐ Get your head dress and veil ready for the hairdresser tomorrow.

☐ Keep an hour free for deep relaxation or a massage.

☐ Take some time out with the people closest to you.

☐ Get an early night.

CONTROLLING YOUR COUNTDOWN

From now on, you'll be updating your countdown regularly (see the checklist on page 187). At the beginning it will be monthly, then weekly and, in the last couple of weeks, you'll be referring to it every day:

♦ Tick or cross of the items that are completed or underway.

♦ Make a note to remind yourself about any items you haven't got around to yet.

♦ Add all the items that arise as the grand plan unfolds.

And, if you're feeling overwhelmed, you can relax. In Chapter 12 you'll find the contact details you need for every single step of the countdown.

$\textcircled{12}$

Useful Addresses, Telephone Numbers and Websites

GENERAL WEDDING INFORMATION

Bridal shows

Silverlinings: 01832 731173/www.silverlinings.co.uk
Terry Burns Wedding Fairs (Ireland): 00353 (0) 1 4901405
The London Wedding Show: www.wedding-expo.com
UK Wedding Show at Wembley: 01704 833207
Wedding Fayres: 01625 610004/www.weddingfayres.co.uk

Websites

www.bride2b.co.uk
www.confetti.co.uk
www.getspliced.com
www.hitched.co.uk
www.irishweddingsonline.com
www.kodakweddings.com
www.scottishweddings.org
www.scottishweddingsonline.com
www.theusefulweddingsite.co.uk
www.ulsterweddingsonline.com
www.webwedding.co.uk
www.weddingguideuk.com
www.wedding-pages.co.uk
www.wedding-service.co.uk

www.weddings.co.uk
www.weddingrealm.com
www.weddingservices4u.co.uk
www.wedseek.co.uk
www.welshweddingsonline.com

Wedding co-ordinators
If you decide to use a wedding co-ordinator, be sure to negotiate their fee and exactly what it includes. Insist on checking references.

Milestone Weddings: 020 8488 7223/
    www.milestoneweddings.co.uk
The Wedding Event Company: 01536 744141/
    www.theweddingeventcompany.co.uk
Virgin Brides: 020 7766 9102/0161 829 8900/
    www.virgin.com/brides

Insurance
E & L: 08707 423580/www.weddinginsurance.org
Jackson Emms & Co. Ltd (Kodak Weddings): 0800 783
    7492
Wedding Plan Insurance: 01603 463099

THE WEDDING

Religious weddings
Baptist Union of Great Britain
Baptist House
129 Broadway
Didcot OX11 8RT
01235 512077/517700

Buddhist: London Buddhist Vihara: 020 8995 9493

Catholic Church
Catholic Marriage Care
Clitherow House
1 Blythe Mews
Blythe Road
London W14 0NW
020 7371 1341

Church of England
The Registrar of the Court of Faculties
1 The Sanctuary
London SW1P 3JT
020 7222 5381/020 7898 1000
www.cofe.anglican.org

Church of Scotland: 0131 225 5722

Greek Archdiocese: 020 7723 4787

Jewish Marriage Council
23 Ravenshurst Avenue
London NW4 4EE
020 8203 6311
Office of the Chief Rabbi: 020 8343 6314

Methodist Church Press Office
Westminster Central Hall
Storey's Gate
London SW1H 9NH
020 7222 8010

Religious Society of Friends (Quakers)
Friends House
173–177 Euston Road
London NW1 2BJ
020 7387 3601

United Reformed Church
86 Tavistock Place
London WC1H 9RT
020 7916 2020

Non-religious weddings
British Humanist Association
47 Theobald's Road
London WC1X 8SP
020 7430 0908/0870 516 8122/ www.humanism.org.uk/
info@humanism.org.uk

Alternative Celebrations: 023 8086 1256

www.afterhoursuk.com (alternative weddings throughout
the UK)

Civil weddings
General Register Office for England and Wales
Marriages Section
General Register Office
Smedley Hydro
Trafalgar Road
Southport PR8 2HH
0870 243 7788/www.statistics.gov.uk/registration

For a full list of licensed venues call ONS: 0151 471 4458
   (£5)
ONS (Office for National Statistics)
Local Services
PO Box 56
Southport PR8 2GL
0151 471 4817/local.services@ons.gov.uk

General Register Office for Guernsey: 01481 725277
General Register Office for Northern Ireland: 028 9025
   2000
General Register Office for Scotland: 0131 314 4447

Weddings abroad and honeymoons
www.weddingsabroad.com
Weddings & Honeymoons Abroad:
   www.weddings-abroad.com/0161 969 1122
www.wedding-manual.co.uk

British Airways Holidays: 01293 722727
Caribtours: 020 7741 0660
Carrier Tailormade Holidays: 01625 582881
First Choice: 0161 742 2262
Hayes & Jarvis: 020 8222 7830
Kuoni: 020 7589 8958
Owners' Syndicate: 020 7801 9801
Sandals: 020 7581 9895
Thomson: 01509 238000
Tropical Places: 0870 444 0692

SHOWERS, HEN PARTIES AND STAG NIGHTS

Parties
Bash: 020 7624 1432/www.yourbash.co.uk

Action breaks and days out
Daytona Raceway offers Grand-Prix style racing in go-karts followed by a meal and drinks at the bar afterwards: 0500 145155

Anglian Activity Breaks – everything from motor boating and paintballing to tank driving and survival courses: 01603 700706

Red Letter Days – wide range of activities including hot-air ballooning, white-water rafting and stock-car racing: 020 8343 5354

Jim Russell Racing Drivers School at Donnington Park: 01332 811430

Action weekend of 4 × 4 off road driving in Ireland: 00 35361 368809

The Adventure Company for activity weekends: 01768 775351

Weekends
Aer Lingus Holidays for breaks in Dublin: 020 8569 4001

Best Western Hotels for speciality weekend breaks: 020 8541 0050

Crystal Holidays for weekend breaks and European cities: 020 8390 9900

Grand Heritage Hotels for weekend breaks: 020 7376 1777

Moswin Tours for beer festivals and European weekend breaks: 0116 271 4982

Orient Express Hotels and Trains: 020 7928 6000

MUSIC
Absolute Musicians: 020 8530 6900/020 8558 0977
Choice Music: www.choicemusic.co.uk
Function Junction: 01932 843384/
    www.functionjunction.co.uk
Little Gem Productions: 07887 986 074/
    www.littlegemproductions.com
Music at Your Service: 01905 358474
Music Finders: 01273 603633
Organisation: 07050 205588 (organists)
Seraphim Trumpets: 01737 814831
Stemberg Clarke: 020 8877 1102 (organised the music for
    the Beckham wedding)
The Wedding Music Company: 020 8293 3392 (church
    music)

FLOWERS
British Retail and Professional Florists Association:
    01942 719127

PHOTOGRAPHY
Before you hire a photographer, ask to see his or her
portfolio and ask what sort of deal he or she is offering.
Don't agree to something that leaves you very little choice
having to select 20 photographs out of a total of only 24,
for example, would not give you enough choice.

Guild of Wedding Photographers: 01225 760088/
    www.gwp-uk.co.uk

The photographs used for this book were supplied by
David and Beverley Foster. Visit David's website at
www.weddingphotovideo.com and Beverley's at

www.weddingstorybook.co.uk

THE CAKE
British Sugarcraft Guild: 020 8859 6943/www.bsguk.org

THE WEDDING LIST

Co-ordinators
Trading Direct: 01672 516633
Wedding List Services: 020 7978 1118

Store lists
Allders: 020 8256 7000/www.allders.co.uk
Argos: 01908 600557
Confetti: 0870 840 6060/wwwlconffeti.co.uk
Debenhams: 020 7580 3000/www.debenhams.com
Harrods: 020 7225 6500
Heals: 020 7636 1666 (ext 246)
House of Fraser: 020 7963 2000
John Lewis: 0845 600 2202
Liberty: 020 7734 1234
Marks & Spencer: 01925 858502
Selfridges: 020 7318 3395
Wrapit: 020 8875 8857/www.wrapit.co.uk

WEDDING CLOTHES
There are so many places to go for your wedding dress, your bridesmaids' dresses and all the accessories that it's best to do your own research on this. Buy the current crop of wedding magazines and start looking through them.

FORMAL SUITS FOR THE GROOM, BEST MAN AND USHERS

If the men in the wedding party are wearing morning dress, they have less of a choice. Most towns have at least one formal dress-hire shop and the following ones have branches all over the UK.

Formal Affair: 01827 261155/www.formalaffair.co.uk
(Wales, central and northern England)
Hugh Harris: 0800 074 9153/www.flashharris.co.uk/
www.hughharris.co.uk (nationwide)
Young's: 020 8327 2731/www.youngs-hire.co.uk (nation-
wide)

HAIR AND BEAUTY TREATMENTS

Make-up lessons

All these cosmetic companies offer make-up lessons at most of their shops and in-store counters in the UK and Ireland. Some of them do special bridal make-overs and a home make-up service on the wedding day.

Bobbi Brown: 01730 232566
The Body Shop: 01903 731500
Chanel also offers a make-up service but inquiries should be made directly at the counter
Christian Dior: 01273 615400
Clarins: 020 7307 6700
Clinique: 020 7409 6951
Elizabeth Arden – inquire at the counter
Estee Lauder: 0800 525501
Givenchy: 020 7563 8800
Guerlain: inquire at the counter; some of them offer the

service and some don't
Helena Rubinstein: 01737 741000
Lancome – ask directly at the counter
MAC: 020 7534 9222
Max Factor: 0800 169 1302
MEA: 020 7408 4444
Molton Brown: 020 7625 6550
Nina Ricci: 020 7499 4420
No 7 (Boots) ask at the large stores and Wellbeing centres
Space NK: 020 7299 4999
Virgin Vie: 0845 300 8022

Hair salons with bridal services
Aberdeen Ishoka: 01224 641900
Brighton Ash Hairdressing: 01273 747441
Bristol Style Collection (Downend): 0117 956 9287;(Clifton): 0117 973 8373
Cardiff Ocean, Roath: 029 2046 5551
Edinburgh Medusa: 0131 225 6627
Glasgow JR's (Cardonald): 0141 883 9283; (Dennistoun): 0141 554 4471; Ibrox: 0141 427 5351; (Kelvinside): 0141 946 4336; (Mosspark): 0141 883 8893; (Scotstoun): 0141 954 3705; Rainbow Room International, George Square: 0141 226 3451
Hampshire Garbo's Hair & Beauty (Southsea): 023 9275 5520; (Portsmouth): 023 9267 8460; Hair OTT, (Cosham): 023 9221 4040; (Portsmouth): 023 9282 4117
Hertfordshire HOB (Hair On Broadway), (Bushey Heath): 020 8950 1515; (Radlett): 01923 850505
Humberside The Mark Hill Salon, Hull: 01482 656424
Kent Capelli, Tonbridge: 01732 358877
Leicestershire Minarik, Kibworth: 0116 279 2529

Lincolnshire Cutting Club, Cleethorpes: 01472 694900

Liverpool Barbara Daley Hair & Beauty: 0151 709 7974

London Errol Douglas, Belgravia: 020 7235 0110; Redhed, Charlotte Place: 020 7436 8099; Robert Ari Hair, Whetstone: 020 8446 8811

Manchester Razor's Edge: 0161 832 7798

Middlesex HOB (Hair On Broadway) (Northwood): 01923 828888; (Stanmore): 020 8954 5991

Newcastle upon Tyne Hooker & Young, Marriot Hotel, High Gosforth Park: 0191 217 0217

West Midlands Royston Blythe, Wolverhampton: 01902 751720

Pampering weekends

Bodysgallen Hall
Llandudno, North Wales
01492 584466

Burleigh Springs
Loughborough, Leicestershire
01509 633016

Cedar Falls
Bishop's Lydeard, Somerset
01823 433233

The Celtic Manor
Newport, Gwent
01633 413000

Champneys
Tring, Hertfordshire
01442 291000

Clarice House
Bury St Edmunds, Suffolk
01284 705550

The Dorchester Spa
London
020 7495 7335

Elizabeth Arden Red Door Spa
London
020 7629 4488

Henlow Grange
Bedfordshire
01462 811111

Hoar Cross Hall
Staffordshire
01283 576515

Inchydoney Island Lodge & Spa
West Cork, Ireland
00353 23 33143

Malmaison
Manchester: 0161 278 1000
Newcastle: 0191 245 5000

Ragdale Hall
Leicestershire
01664 434831

Rowhill Grange
Dartford, Kent
01322 615136

The Sanctuary
London
0870 063 0300

Stobo Castle
Peebles-shire
01721 760249

Wedding Countdown Checklist

You might like to use the following as a checklist for the countdown to your wedding. It is based on those things discussed more fully in Chapter 11. Inevitably, however, there will be some things included in this checklist that are not applicable to your own wedding plans, as well as some things relevant to you that are missing. You could, therefore, cross out those things not relevant to you and use the blank spaces in the checklist to add any items that have not been included.

◆ Tick or cross off items that are completed/underway. Make a note to remind yourself of any items you haven't got round to yet or that need chasing up at a later date.

◆ Add any extra items that arise in the blank spaces provided.

◆ You could perhaps use the 'Notes' sections to remind yourself of the more urgent things.

◆ You could use the 'Budget' sections for those (perhaps unforeseen) things that arise that will have a major impact on the budget you have already allocated.

◆ It might also be as well to keep an eye on the months as these pass by. You could, therefore, add the relevant month after the heading 'Six months before', etc.

AS SOON AS YOU DECIDE TO GET MARRIED

Tick if done/underway

Have you:

Set a provisional date for the wedding? ☐

Told all the important people in your life? ☐

Decided on what sort of ceremony you want? ☐

Contacted the appropriate people about
the ceremony? ☐

Checked the legal requirements for your
type of ceremony? ☐

Contacted anyone who might want to help pay
for the wedding? ☐

Drawn up a tentative guest list? ☐

Agreed on the budget? ☐

Checked out the reception venue you want? ☐

Thought about whether you want to arrange it
all yourself or whether you'd like a wedding
co-ordinator? ☐

Planned your honeymoon? ☐

Provisionally booked your first-night hotel
room or bridal suite? ☐

Taken out wedding insurance? ☐

The bride's checklist

Have you:

Started reading magazines and looking at websites
to give you ideas about your ceremony,
your reception and, of course, the dress? ☐

Started a file on everything from your shoes to
the cake, cutting out everything that you like? ☐

Thought about your wedding dress? ☐

Made appointments to start trying wedding
dresses on? ☐

Notes

Budget

SIX MONTHS BEFORE

Month:

Tick if done/underway

Have you:

Sent out your pre-invitations? ☐

Confirmed all the major arrangements? ☐

Booked the photographer? ☐

Ordered the cake? ☐

Hired the entertainment for the reception? ☐

Chosen, inspected and hired your wedding
transport? ☐

Ordered the wedding stationery? ☐

Chosen your wedding support team? ☐

Thought about what the men in the wedding
party are going to wear and, if necessary,
made arrangements to hire or buy their
outfits? ☐

Booked the florist? ☐

Arranged crèche facilities? ☐

Chosen your wedding rings? ☐

Put your wedding-gift list together? ☐

If you're going abroad for your honeymoon,
checked your passports are valid? ☐

The bride's checklist

Have you:

Chosen your dress and your bridesmaid's
dresses? □

Begun your pre-wedding beauty routine? □

Started exercising if you need to get into shape? □

Promised yourself you'll eat healthy food from
now on and that you'll drink plenty of water? □

Experimented with your hair and make-up? □

Notes

Budget

THREE MONTHS BEFORE

Month:

Tick if done/underway

Have you:

Called the first meeting of your wedding
    support team? ☐

Drawn up your final guest list, based on the
    responses to your pre-invitations? ☐

Sent out the invitations? ☐

Decided on the wedding menu and wine? ☐

Confirmed the wedding-cake design? ☐

Confirmed the music for the venue and decided
    what to do about the first dance? ☐

Confirmed the details of your wedding
    ceremony? ☐

Confirmed the flowers you will need? ☐

If you are having a register office wedding,
    confirmed by it now? ☐

Finalised your honeymoon plans and found out
    about vaccinations and visas? ☐

Checked that the male members of the wedding
    team have their suits and accessories
    organised? ☐

The bride's checklist

Have you:

Discussed hair style with your hairdresser? ☐

Arranged for a trial run for your make-up? ☐

Bought shoes and accessories for yourself and
    your bridesmaids? ☐

Bought your going-away outfit? ☐

Liaised with both mothers on their choices of
    outfits and colours? ☐

Notes

Budget

TWO MONTHS BEFORE

Month:

Tick if done/underway

Have you:

Arranged for the best man and chief
bridesmaid to organise the stag night and
hen party? ☐

Sent out wedding-present lists to anyone who
requests them? ☐

Started a list of the wedding gifts you receive
and marked up the ones who have already
had thank-you letters? ☐

Made sure all the guests have somewhere to
stay and booked accommodation for them if
necessary? ☐

Bought any little bits and pieces you might
want for your reception? ☐

Written the speeches and practised them? ☐

The bride's checklist

Have you:

If you're planning to use your husband's name
at all, informed banks, credit card companies,
employer, doctor and dentist? ☐

Bought gifts for the bridesmaids and your
fiancé? ☐

Liaised with your fiancé to buy gifts for the
best man and ushers? ☐

Notes

Budget

ONE MONTH BEFORE

Month:

Tick if done/underway

Have you:

Called a meeting of the wedding support team? ☐

Chased up any guests who haven't replied to
their invitations? ☐

Let the reception venue and caterers know the
final numbers? ☐

Checked that the outfits for the wedding party
are all organised? ☐

At the same time and day of the week as the
wedding, arranged to have a practice run
from the bride's house to the wedding venue? ☐

Drawn up your table plan? ☐

Checked the order of ceremony sheets, menus
and place cards have been delivered? ☐

The bride's checklist

Have you:

Made the personal appointments you'll need for yourself and your bridesmaids?	☐
Started your tanning sessions if you're planning to have them?	☐
Collected your dress?	☐
Checked your wedding outfit is complete?	☐
Checked the bridesmaids' outfits are complete?	☐
Bought your going-away outfit and honeymoon clothes?	☐

Notes

Budget

TWO WEEKS BEFORE

Date:

Tick if done/underway

Have you confirmed everything:

Ceremony? ☐

Reception? ☐

Cake? ☐

Flowers? ☐

Transport? ☐

Honeymoon and first-night accommodation? ☐

Have you:

Ordered your foreign currency for the
   honeymoon? ☐

Made a list of telephone numbers in case
   of an emergency on the day? ☐

The bride's checklist

Have you:

Worn your wedding shoes around the house?   ☐

Stepped up the beauty routine?   ☐

Notes

Budget

ONE WEEK BEFORE

Date:

Tick if done/underway

Have you called the final pre-wedding meeting of the support team and checked that:

Everyone knows what he or she is doing? ☐

Everyone's got everything he or she needs? ☐

Somebody is going to collect the wedding
  presents after the reception? ☐

Somebody is going to return any outfits that
  have been hired? ☐

Have you:

Arranged the final rehearsal at the venue for
  the ceremony and also the rehearsal dinner? ☐

Made sure you have as much help as you need
  immediately before the wedding? ☐

The bride's checklist

Have you:

Made the final arrangements with your bridesmaids?	☐
Double-checked your outfit?	☐

Notes

Budget

THE DAY BEFORE

Tick if done/underway

Have you:

Checked that the best man has the rings? ☐

Spoken to the wedding support team on the
phone if you're not going to be seeing them? ☐

The bride's checklist

Have you:

Eaten some breakfast?	☐
Had your pedicure and manicure if you aren't having them on the morning?	☐
Packed your clothes for after the wedding and arranged for them to be taken to the reception or first-night hotel?	☐
Got your head dress and veil ready for the hairdresser tomorrow?	☐
Kept an hour free for deep relaxation or a massage?	☐
Taken some time out with the people closest to you?	☐
Planned for an early night?	☐

Notes

Budget

Index